GLOBAL
WARMING

OPPOSING VIEWPOINTS®

Other Books of Related Interest

Opposing Viewpoints Series

Africa
America Beyond 2001
Central America
Endangered Species
The Environment
Global Resources
Population
Poverty
The Third World
Trade
21st Century Earth
Water

Current Controversies Series

Energy Alternatives
Hunger
Pollution

At Issue Series

Environmental Justice

GLOBAL WARMING

OPPOSING VIEWPOINTS®

David Bender & Bruno Leone, *Series Editors*

Tamara L. Roleff, *Book Editor*
Scott Barbour and Karin L. Swisher,
   Assistant Editors

OPPOSING
VIEWPOINTS®
SERIES

Greenhaven Press, Inc., San Diego, CA

Photo credit: Clement Mok

Greenhaven Press, Inc.
PO Box 289009
San Diego, CA 92198-9009

Library of Congress Cataloging-in-Publication Data

Global warming : opposing viewpoints / Tamara L. Roleff, book editor, Scott Barbour, assistant editor, Karin L. Swisher, assistant editor.
    p.   cm. — (Opposing viewpoints series)
Includes bibliographical references and index.
ISBN 1-56510-512-5 (lib. bdg. : alk. paper). —
ISBN 1-56510-511-7 (pbk. : alk. paper)
   1. Global warming. I. Roleff, Tamara L., 1959–   .
II. Barbour, Scott, 1963–   . III. Swisher, Karin, 1966–   .
IV. Series: Opposing viewpoints series (Unnumbered)
QC981.8.G56G581945   1997
363.73'87—dc20
                                                  96-25705
                                                      CIP

Every effort has been made to trace the owners of copyrighted material.

"Congress shall make no law . . . abridging the freedom of speech, or of the press."

First Amendment to the U.S. Constitution

The basic foundation of our democracy is the First Amendment guarantee of freedom of expression. The Opposing Viewpoints Series is dedicated to the concept of this basic freedom and the idea that it is more important to practice it than to enshrine it.

Contents

Chapter 4: Should Measures Be Taken to Combat Global Warming?

Chapter 5: How Can the Rain Forests Be Preserved?

Why Consider Opposing Viewpoints?

"The only way in which a human being can make some approach to knowing the whole of a subject is by hearing what can be said about it by persons of every variety of opinion and studying all modes in which it can be looked at by every character of mind. No wise man ever acquired his wisdom in any mode but this."

John Stuart Mill

In our media-intensive culture it is not difficult to find differing opinions. Thousands of newspapers and magazines and dozens of radio and television talk shows resound with differing points of view. The difficulty lies in deciding which opinion to agree with and which "experts" seem the most credible. The more inundated we become with differing opinions and claims, the more essential it is to hone critical reading and thinking skills to evaluate these ideas. Opposing Viewpoints books address this problem directly by presenting stimulating debates that can be used to enhance and teach these skills. The varied opinions contained in each book examine many different aspects of a single issue. While examining these conveniently edited opposing views, readers can develop critical thinking skills such as the ability to compare and contrast authors' credibility, facts, argumentation styles, use of persuasive techniques, and other stylistic tools. In short, the Opposing Viewpoints Series is an ideal way to attain the higher-level thinking and reading skills so essential in a culture of diverse and contradictory opinions.

In addition to providing a tool for critical thinking, Opposing Viewpoints books challenge readers to question their own strongly held opinions and assumptions. Most people form their opinions on the basis of upbringing, peer pressure, and personal, cultural, or professional bias. By reading carefully balanced opposing views, readers must directly confront new ideas as well as the opinions of those with whom they disagree. This is not to simplistically argue that everyone who reads opposing views will—or should—change his or her opinion. Instead, the series enhances readers' depth of understanding of their own views by encouraging confrontation with opposing ideas. Careful examination of others' views can lead to the readers' understanding of the logical inconsistencies in their own opinions, perspective on why they hold an opinion, and the consideration of the possibility that their opinion requires further evaluation.

Evaluating Other Opinions

To ensure that this type of examination occurs, Opposing Viewpoints books present all types of opinions. Prominent spokespeople on different sides of each issue as well as well-known professionals from many disciplines challenge the reader. An additional goal of the series is to provide a forum for other, less known, or even unpopular viewpoints. The opinion of an ordinary person who has had to make the decision to cut off life support from a terminally ill relative, for example, may be just as valuable and provide just as much insight as a medical ethicist's professional opinion. The editors have two additional purposes in including these less known views. One, the editors encourage readers to respect others' opinions—even when not enhanced by professional credibility. It is only by reading or listening to and objectively evaluating others' ideas that one can determine whether they are worthy of consideration. Two, the inclusion of such viewpoints encourages the important critical thinking skill of objectively evaluating an author's credentials and bias. This evaluation will illuminate an author's reasons for taking a particular stance on an issue and will aid in readers' evaluation of the author's ideas.

As series editors of the Opposing Viewpoints Series, it is our hope that these books will give readers a deeper understanding of the issues debated and an appreciation of the complexity of even seemingly simple issues when good and honest people disagree. This awareness is particularly important in a democratic society such as ours in which people enter into public debate to determine the common good. Those with whom one disagrees should not be regarded as enemies but rather as people whose views deserve careful examination and may shed light on one's own.

Thomas Jefferson once said that "difference of opinion leads to inquiry, and inquiry to truth." Jefferson, a broadly educated man, argued that "if a nation expects to be ignorant and free . . . it expects what never was and never will be." As individuals and as a nation, it is imperative that we consider the opinions of others and examine them with skill and discernment. The Opposing Viewpoints Series is intended to help readers achieve this goal.

David L. Bender & Bruno Leone,
Series Editors

Introduction

"The growing accumulation of manmade gases in the Earth's atmosphere could someday push temperatures to dangerously high levels."

Mark Nichols, Maclean's, April 24, 1995

"Computer studies of the greenhouse effect have exaggerated global warming."

George C. Marshall Institute, 1995

The earth's atmosphere, which extends about five hundred miles into space from the planet's surface, is made up of five layers of gases that act like a blanket to warm the planet. These gases are similar to greenhouse windows: They allow sunlight to pass through to warm the planet's surface and surrounding air, and they hold in most of the solar-generated heat. For this reason, carbon dioxide, methane, ozone, and water vapor, among other atmospheric gases, are called greenhouse gases. The process by which these gases capture and absorb the reflected solar energy is known as the greenhouse effect. Without the greenhouse effect, the planet would be inhospitable to life because the earth's surface temperature would be cooler by about 63°F.

During the 1970s, some scientists began to worry about the greenhouse effect when they realized that the average surface temperature of the earth had risen nearly 1°F during the twentieth century. Many researchers, including James E. Hansen, director of NASA's Goddard Institute for Space Studies, blame this enhanced greenhouse effect on human causes. They argue that the burning of wood and fossil fuels such as natural gas, oil, and coal has released large amounts of carbon dioxide into the atmosphere. Because carbon dioxide is a greenhouse gas, these researchers maintain, an increased concentration of this gas has resulted in the trapping of more heat, thereby causing the atmospheric temperature to rise. If steps are not taken to reduce emissions of carbon dioxide into the atmosphere, Hansen and other scientists contend, the yearly emissions rate will increase nearly 50 percent from six billion tons in 1995 to nine billion tons by 2010. These researchers estimate that such an increase in carbon dioxide emissions would raise the earth's average surface temperature 2°F to 6°F by 2100.

Some policymakers and scientists believe that the loss of rain forests across the planet contributes to the increase in atmospheric carbon dioxide. The destruction of the forests is a double blow for the global environment, they maintain. According to these experts, the rain forests serve as "sinks" for atmospheric carbon dioxide by absorbing the greenhouse gas and releasing oxygen in its place during photosynthesis. Deforestation allows the carbon dioxide that would have been absorbed by the trees to remain in the atmosphere, they assert. In addition, these scientists contend, when the trees decay or burn, carbon dioxide that was previously absorbed by the trees is released back into the atmosphere. According to George M. Woodwell and Kilaparti Ramakrishna of the Woods Hole Research Center, "Deforestation is the second biggest source of carbon dioxide, . . . only the burning of oil, coal and gas produce more. . . . If [global warming] is to be slowed, the world must not only stop cutting and burning large forests, but replace many millions of acres that have been destroyed."

However, not everyone agrees that global warming is due to manmade causes. For instance, in 1991 two Danish researchers, Eigil Friis-Christensen and Knud Lassen, presented their findings that the length of sunspot cycles seems to affect the earth's average surface temperature. The length of the sunspot cycle—the period in which the number of sunspots changes from most to least, or vice versa—averages about eleven years, with variations from nine to thirteen years. Friis-Christensen and Lassen discovered that the earth's average global temperature tends to warm during a short sunspot cycle while a long cycle brings cooler temperatures. This suggests, these researchers conclude, that the sunspot cycle variations explain much of the temperature changes blamed on global warming.

Another possible natural cause of global warming is the weather phenomenon known as El Niño. El Niño is a warm ocean current that periodically appears off the coast of Peru and Ecuador from December through March; the term is also commonly used to refer to the current's sporadic long-term effects of drought and severe storms throughout the Pacific region. Nicholas E. Graham of the Scripps Institute of Oceanography in La Jolla, California, maintains that there is a link between El Niño and rising global temperatures. According to Graham, computer models show that unusually frequent patterns of El Niño's warm current in the tropical Pacific waters have caused the ocean and atmospheric temperatures to rise, thus warming the globe.

Not only are scientists divided on the causes of global warming, they also do not agree on the impact that global warming will have on the earth. Some researchers and policymakers contend that global warming will have a disastrous effect on the world's environment. The increase in global warmth will cause the ocean temperatures to rise, they maintain, killing off the phytoplankton, oceanic plants that need cold water temperatures to survive. The loss of phytoplankton will not only affect the marine food chains, these scientists assert, but will also reduce the amount of oceanic vegetation that can absorb carbon dioxide. In addition, they argue, warmer ocean temperatures will melt the world's ice caps and glaciers, causing sea levels to rise and flooding in many low-lying cities, countries, and islands. Rodolfo del Valle of the Argentine Antarctic Institute blamed global warming for causing a 48-by-22-mile chunk of Antarctica's Larsen Ice Shelf to break off in 1994, ten years earlier than predicted. The break exposed rocks that had been covered for twenty-thousand years.

The effects of global warming will also be felt on land, these researchers assert. In the mid-latitudes, they believe, the warmer temperatures will dry out the soil and cause droughts, increase the risk of wildfires, and allow insect pests to multiply and extend their ranges. Furthermore, some scientists maintain, hurricanes and other storms will become more frequent and severe. "As you get more global warming, you should see an increase in the extremes of the hydrologic cycle—droughts and floods and heavy precipitation," argues Hansen.

Other scientists maintain that such predictions of global disaster are not supported by research. Skeptics emphasize the inadequacy of the computer models used to predict future trends in global warming, the scientific uncertainty about the relationship between clouds and global warming, and the lack of knowledge concerning the exchange of carbon dioxide between the atmosphere and the oceans.

These skeptical scientists question the assertion that temperatures could rise 6°F in the next one hundred years. Richard S. Lindzen, a professor of meteorology at the Massachusetts Institute of Technology, testified at an environmental hearing in St. Paul, Minnesota, in 1994 that a doubling of carbon emissions during the twenty-first century would probably warm the atmosphere no more than .5°F. Robert C. Balling Jr., director of the Office of Climatology at Arizona State University, argued at the same hearing that the average global temperature should rise no more than 2°F. S. Fred Singer, director of the Science and Environmental Policy Project, maintains that satellite data actually show a slight cooling trend in global temperatures.

Moreover, these researchers assert, if the earth's average temperature does increase dramatically, the warmer temperatures will be beneficial for most regions of the planet since it is probable that only the nights will become warmer while daytime temperatures will remain the same. If nighttime temperatures rise, they contend, it is unlikely that the number and severity of droughts will increase. Because the higher latitudes will warm the most and equatorial areas the least, they argue, crop growing seasons will lengthen and food production will increase in many areas of the world. For instance, these experts maintain, the northern regions of the United States, Canada, and Russia will become more suitable for growing crops. These are just some examples, the skeptics proclaim, of how global warming will do more good than harm.

Scientists, researchers, and policymakers on both sides of the global warming debate see evidence to support their positions. *Global Warming: Opposing Viewpoints* presents their opinions in the following chapters: Does Global Warming Pose a Serious Threat? What Causes Global Warming? What Will Be the Effects of Global Warming? Should Measures Be Taken to Combat Global Warming? How Can the Rain Forests Be Preserved? This anthology examines the myriad viewpoints shaping the controversy over global warming.

Does Global Warming Pose a Serious Threat?

GLOBAL
WARMING

Chapter Preface

In June 1988, James E. Hansen, director of the Goddard Institute for Space Studies at the National Aeronautics and Space Administration (NASA), told a Senate committee that "the greenhouse effect has been detected and is changing our climate now." With this declaration, Hansen launched an ongoing international debate on the extent of global warming and its potential to adversely affect Earth's environment.

Scientists and environmentalists who agree with Hansen believe that global warming presents a significant threat to the health of the planet. They point out that during the twentieth century, Earth's mean temperature increased by approximately one degree Fahrenheit. Relying on forecasts generated by computer models that simulate Earth's atmosphere, these advocates predict that within the next hundred years, the planet's atmospheric temperature will increase an additional two to seven degrees Fahrenheit. This warming trend, they argue, will result in major climatic disruptions, including floods and droughts, rising sea levels, and a growing number of hurricanes and other destructive storms. "The real danger from global warming . . . ," writes Al Gore, "is that the whole global climate system is likely to be thrown out of whack. . . . As the climate pattern begins to change, so too do the movements of the wind and rain, the floods and droughts, the grasslands and deserts."

Many scientists view such assertions with skepticism. Critics have attacked the science of global warming on various grounds, primarily focusing on the computer models used by atmospheric scientists to predict future warming trends. Computer models, they maintain, are unable to re-create the complexities of climatic processes with a high degree of accuracy. For example, models are incapable of accounting for the effects of clouds and water vapor on atmospheric temperatures. Due to this and other shortcomings, Richard S. Lindzen, a professor of meteorology at the Massachusetts Institute of Technology and a critic of global warming science, concludes that "models are at present experimental tools whose relation to the real world is questionable." Lindzen and others contend that the inadequacy of these models casts serious doubt on forecasts of severe climatic changes due to global warming.

As researchers attempt to determine if global warming is a serious problem, the controversy first launched by James E. Hansen in 1988 continues. In the following chapter, scientists and other commentators debate the validity of global warming science and of predictions of future climate changes.

"It is important that society treat human-induced global warming as a serious global-scale environmental threat."

Global Warming Poses a Serious Threat

Robert T. Watson

Robert T. Watson is associate director for environment in the White House Office of Science and Technology. In the following viewpoint, Watson argues that global warming—which he believes is caused largely by human activities that increase carbon dioxide in the atmosphere—presents a serious environmental threat. He predicts that if current trends continue, the global mean temperature will rise between two and seven degrees Fahrenheit by the year 2100, resulting in floods, droughts, and rising sea levels. These climatic changes, according to Watson, will adversely affect human health, agriculture, and food and water supplies worldwide.

As you read, consider the following questions:

1. By what percentage has the amount of carbon dioxide in the atmosphere increased since 1700, according to Watson?
2. According to the author, how much has the global mean air-surface temperature warmed during the last 100 years?
3. What health problems does Watson say might result from a warmer world?

Robert T. Watson, "Is Man-Made Global Warming a Proven Environmental Threat? Yes: It Bodes Ill for Health, Agriculture, and Biodiversity," *Insight*, September 4, 1995. Reprinted with permission of *Insight*. Copyright 1995 The Washington Times Corporation.

A small, vocal minority of skeptics claims there is no scientific evidence to support the theory that man-made emissions of greenhouse gases will alter the Earth's climate. They claim that global warming is liberal, left-wing, claptrap science and a ploy by the scientific community to ensure funding for yet another "Chicken Little" scare. Others suggest that attempts to reduce greenhouse-gas emissions by changing energy- or land-use policies would needlessly cost the American taxpayer tens to hundreds of billions of dollars annually and that it is really part of an international conspiracy to undermine America's competitiveness in the global marketplace.

The truth, however, is quite different. The overwhelming majority of scientific experts believes human-induced climate change is inevitable. The question is not *whether* climate will change in response to human activities, but rather *where* (regional patterns), *when* (the rate of change) and by *how much* (magnitude). This is the fundamental conclusion of a careful and objective analysis of all relevant scientific, technical and economic information by thousands of experts from academia, governments, industry and environmental organizations under the auspices of the U.N. Intergovernmental Panel on Climate Change.

The view of the majority of scientists is shared by 130 nations, including the United States, that signed and ratified the U.N. Convention on Climate Change. At a meeting in Berlin in March 1995, all parties to the treaty agreed that current actions to mitigate climate change are inadequate to protect society from the threat of human-induced global warming.

The good news is that the majority of energy experts, and energy organizations such as the World Energy Council, believe that dramatic reductions in greenhouse-gas emissions are technically feasible at little or no cost to society due to an array of energy technologies and policy measures. Many of these will have other benefits for society. For example, the use of more energy-efficient buildings and motor vehicles would reduce dependence on the importation of foreign oil and reduce air pollution at the same time. Although significant progress can be made with current technologies, a commitment to further research and development is essential.

Climate Changes

However, we must keep in mind the following points about current scientific understanding of the climate system:

First, human activities undoubtedly are increasing atmospheric concentrations of greenhouse gases, which tend to warm the atmosphere. The most important greenhouse gas directly affected by human activities is carbon dioxide, which has increased by nearly 30 percent since 1700, primarily because of changes in land use (deforestation) and the burning of coal, oil and gas. In some regions of the world, human activities also have increased the atmospheric concentrations of aerosols (tiny airborne particles), which tend to cool the atmosphere.

Second, there is no doubt that the Earth's climate has changed during the last 100 years. The global mean air-surface temperature over the land and ocean has warmed between 0.6 and 1.1 degrees Fahrenheit, glaciers have retreated globally and sea level has risen 10 to 25 centimeters. Since the late 1970s there has been a decrease in Arctic Ocean ice and an unusual persistence of the El Niño conditions in the Pacific Ocean that affect severe weather patterns globally. In addition, the nine warmest years this century have occurred since 1980.

Third, while there has been, as yet, no definitive detection of a human-induced global-warming signal in the climate record, the evidence increasingly points in that direction. Comparing the observed changes in global mean temperature with model simulations that incorporate the effect of increases in greenhouse gases and aerosols suggests that the observed changes during the last century are unlikely to be due entirely to natural causes. This conclusion is strengthened further when the observed regional and vertical patterns of temperature changes are compared to those expected from human activities. This similarity in patterns suggests that the temperature record is reflecting human activities. In addition, the increase in the frequency of heavy rains in the United States is yet another signal consistent with human-induced global warming.

Future Trends

Fourth, assuming no climate-change policies, emissions of carbon dioxide and other greenhouse gases are bound to increase. For example, emissions of carbon dioxide in the year 2100 could range from about 6 billion tons per year, similar to current emissions, to as high as 36 billion tons per year. Such emissions would lead to carbon-dioxide concentrations ranging from three to eight times the preindustrial levels and still increasing rapidly. Climate models suggest that these projected emissions in greenhouse gases and aerosols would lead to an increase in the global mean temperature of 2 to 7 degrees Fahrenheit by 2100, the swiftest such rise in the last 10,000 years.

Fifth, these projected temperature changes would be accompanied by changes in the patterns and intensity of rainfall, with an increased tendency for floods and droughts and an increase in sea level of 10 to 120 centimeters by 2100.

Many people, especially those who live in colder climes, question whether we should care if the climate becomes warmer. The answer is quite simple: A warmer climate will be accompanied by changes in precipitation, floods, droughts, heat waves and rises in sea level. Some scientists also worry about changes in the frequency and intensity of tornadoes, cyclones and hurricanes, but their concern is much more speculative.

Predictions of an Arctic Thaw

If predictions of a "greenhouse effect" prove out, then global warming will hit the Arctic faster and harder than anywhere else on Earth. While the planet is widely expected to warm by about 3 to 5.5 degrees Fahrenheit by the year 2050, the Arctic is expected to warm by as much as 18 degrees Fahrenheit, particularly during the winter.

Such an Arctic thaw could devastate the fragile and little-understood ecosystems of the Far North. . . . While no one can say with certainty just what an Arctic thaw would look like, scientists say it could involve anything from the demise of the mighty polar bear to a rise in sea levels and the inundation of dozens of Inuit, or Eskimo, villages that now cling to the Arctic coast.

Some climatologists predict that if large areas of peat-rich Arctic permafrost melt, the thawing soil will release even more greenhouse gases into the atmosphere, accelerating the warming of the rest of the globe.

Still other scholars suggest, paradoxically, that by increasing Arctic seawater evaporation and creating prime conditions for more snow, an Arctic warming could eventually produce a new Ice Age.

Mary Williams Walsh, *Los Angeles Times*, February 8, 1993.

Granted, modern societies have evolved to coexist with today's climate and its natural variability. But even technologically sophisticated nations fall victim to unusual weather woes. Every year throughout the world, thousands die, hundreds of thousands are made homeless and billions of dollars are lost because of floods, droughts, tornadoes, cyclones and hurricanes. Every year since the mid-1980s, the United States has faced a major weather-related disaster, costing lives and an average loss of $1 billion per week. Recall the drought of 1988, Hurricane Andrew of 1992 and the Mississippi River and California floods of 1993 and 1995. Chicago and other American cities [experienced a] deadly heat wave in July 1995, which claimed hundreds of lives—mostly the young and the elderly.

True, climate change would be a boon to some regions of the world, but it could adversely affect those things we care about most: human health, food and water supplies, economic growth and national security.

For example, a warmer world could lead to an increase in vector-borne diseases such as malaria and yellow fever in tropical countries. Add to this an increase in the incidence of heat-stress mortality similar to the effects of the July 1995 heat wave. Agricultural production would suffer in some regions, particularly in developing countries in the tropics and subtropics, even though the effect of climate change on global food production might be small. A rise in sea level would wash away human habitat for millions of people, triggering floods of environmental refugees. Without a doubt the United States will hear calls for increased defense and foreign-aid expenditures to cope with massive displacements of peoples in certain developing countries. Plants and animals will be hit too: A shift in the boundaries of many ecosystems (forests and grasslands, for example) likely will diminish biological diversity, an important source of food, fibre and medicines.

Prudent Actions Required

While it is important that society treat human-induced global warming as a serious global-scale environmental threat requiring concerted global action, there is no reason to panic or take draconian measures. Timely, prudent actions will allow us to slow global warming and develop mitigation and adaptation options without serious economic dislocation. So the question is: How do we rationally deal with the threat of human-induced global warming?

We began when President Bush signed (and the Senate ratified) the Climate Convention, the primary goal of which is the "stabilization of greenhouse-gas concentrations in the atmosphere at a level that would prevent dangerous human-induced interference with the climate system." The treaty specifies that such a stabilization should be achieved within a period sufficient to allow ecosystems to adapt naturally to climate change without endangering food production or economic development.

The United States can pursue this goal without sacrificing our economic competitiveness, or even destroying it, as some have suggested. This would require utilizing better energy-efficiency technologies (both supply and demand), initiating a switch to modern renewable energies such as wind, solar power and bio-fuels, improving the fuel efficiency of vehicles and improving management of agricultural lands, rangelands and forests. Such actions would reduce our energy bills, dependence upon foreign oil and congestion in our streets. The same steps would enhance rural development, improve air quality and reduce soil erosion. These actions would make sense even if there were no threat of global warming.

This is a global problem, hence it requires global solutions.

These solutions provide American industry with opportunities to provide low-emission greenhouse-gas technologies to the rest of the world and become the market leader. If U.S. industry fails to invest in the required research and development of these technologies, we will end up importing them from Germany and Japan.

Policymakers are faced with responding to the risks posed by human-induced emissions of greenhouse gases in the face of scientific uncertainties, particularly with respect to accurate predictions of the magnitude, rate and regional patterns of climate change, but this is no excuse to ignore the problem. Decisions made during the next few years are particularly important because climate-induced environmental changes cannot be reversed for decades, if not millennia.

"Do we face a looming catastrophe? In fact the answer is No."

Global Warming Does Not Pose a Serious Threat

Jeffrey Salmon

In the following viewpoint, Jeffrey Salmon argues that global warming does not pose a significant threat to human health or the environment. He contends that alarms about the potential magnitude and negative consequences of global warming have been based on questionable scientific findings. According to Salmon, environmentalists and politicians have seized on these findings and have promoted a sense of crisis in order to further their own agendas. Salmon is executive director of the George C. Marshall Institute in Washington, D.C., an organization that conducts scientific research on issues that affect public policy.

As you read, consider the following questions:

1. What would be the costs of a 20 percent reduction in CO_2 emissions by the year 2000, according to Salmon?
2. In the author's opinion, why are computer models of climate change unreliable?
3. How was global warming in the 1980s exaggerated by the models used by the Intergovernmental Panel on Climate Change, according to Salmon?

Excerpted from Jeffrey Salmon, "Greenhouse Anxiety." Reprinted from the July 1993 issue of *Commentary*, by permission; all rights reserved.

Of all the environmental calamities that might be visited on the earth, none has attracted more attention or aroused more fear than global warming. Countless newspaper and television reports have warned us that mankind is altering the earth's delicate thermostat by spewing tons of carbon dioxide (CO_2) into the atmosphere, mainly by burning coal and oil. According to the global-warming theory, CO_2—along with other man-made gases such as methane—will enhance the earth's natural "greenhouse effect" to the point of an uncontrollable temperature rise, leaving civilization reeling under the double punishment of farmland drought and catastrophic flooding caused by melting polar ice caps.

On the face of it, the greenhouse effect would seem to be an unlikely candidate for the apocalypse. After all, most predictions suggest the earth's temperature might increase by only a few tenths of a degree per decade, and everyone knows forecasting the weather more than a day ahead is a hit-or-miss proposition. Why then should we take seriously weather predictions years into the future? . . .

A Serious Agenda

The environmental lobby . . . has a . . . serious agenda in mind. Dramatically increased automobile fuel efficiency, and indeed the eventual phasing-out of the internal-combustion engine; carbon taxes; the ultimate elimination of coal- and oil-fired energy production; binding international agreements to reduce carbon-dioxide emissions—these are just a few of the items on the menu of proposed policies. Going even further, the UN Intergovernmental Panel on Climate Change (IPCC) . . . contends that *immediate* reductions of *over 60 percent* in "greenhouse emissions from human activities" are needed just to stabilize CO_2 concentrations at today's levels. Other observers put the figure at closer to 80 percent.

The impact of such numbers is difficult to fathom. According to the Department of Energy, for the U.S. alone, even a 20-percent reduction in CO_2 emissions by the year 2000—the goal President Bill Clinton has committed us to achieving—would require a carbon tax forcing the price of electricity to double, oil prices to triple, and the cost of coal to quintuple. Since the U.S. emits only 30 percent of the earth's greenhouse gases, stabilizing CO_2 emissions worldwide would require much more draconian measures still: it would require a fundamental restructuring of the global economy.

No Catastrophe

Is any of this necessary? Do we face a looming catastrophe? In fact the answer is No. Whatever role might be played by global warming in domestic and international politics, there is *no* solid scientific evidence to support the theory that the earth is warming because of man-made greenhouse gases.

To the contrary, the weight of science indicates that carbon emissions from power plants, cars, and the like have only a marginal impact on the climate. As Robert White, president of the National Academy of Engineering, put it correctly in 1989: "We are confronted with an inverted pyramid of knowledge: a huge and growing mass of proposals for political action is balanced upon a handful of real facts."

How did this happen?

The Science

To understand the political history of global warming it is necessary to begin where the greenhouse argument itself begins, with the science.

The actual greenhouse effect is a natural phenomenon, existing for eons before humans even appeared on the scene. It comes largely from water vapor in the atmosphere which warms the earth by trapping some of the heat from the sun and keeping it in the lower atmosphere. Carbon dioxide, methane, and other gases also trap heat, but most greenhouse heating comes from water vapor. The warming effect of all these gases combined maintains average global temperatures at a comfortable 65°F. Without the greenhouse effect, the average temperature would be about 10° below zero, and the earth would resemble the planet Mars.

So today's ruckus over the greenhouse effect has very little to do with the actual greenhouse effect, which everyone agrees we cannot live without. Instead, the issue concerns the changes that human activities, particularly the burning of fossil fuels, have produced and will produce on the earth's natural climate-control system.

There are many unknowns about that system, but also some generally acknowledged facts. Scientists agree that people have added a great deal of CO_2 to the air over the last 100 years, mostly by driving cars and burning coal and oil for energy. Sometime in the middle of the 21st century we may double the amount of CO_2 in the atmosphere.

Alone, this substantial addition of greenhouse gases might have gone unnoticed by everyone but a handful of experts. Indeed, from the 1940's through the 1970's, while greenhouse gases were pouring into the atmosphere, global temperatures actually fell, and there was much talk in scientific circles about the possibility that we were headed into a new ice age. But this 30-year cooling period interrupted 100 years of generally warmer weather, during which the earth's temperature rose by about 1°F. The global-

25

warming scare rests largely on the coincidence of the global increase in atmospheric CO_2 and this one-degree rise in temperature. (When it comes to global temperature averages, a little can make a great difference—in growing seasons, rainfall, and general weather patterns. But that is a different story.)

The increase in CO_2 in the atmosphere over the last 100 years, the one-degree temperature rise since 1880, the economic impact of climate change—these, too, are not matters of much debate within the scientific community. What scientists wonder about is not whether man-made greenhouse gases influence temperature, but by how much.

Estimates

They have been trying to figure this out for some time. Early estimates, based on a projected doubling of CO_2 in the atmosphere, ranged from as little as 2°F to as much as 10°F. They were regarded as useful experiments, but of limited forecasting value. By the 1960's, though, advances in computer technology gave meteorologists the opportunity to build more sophisticated models using the enormously complex physics which controls weather patterns.

Today's so-called consensus view on global warming, as expressed by the IPCC, suggests that at the current rate of growth in greenhouse gases, average temperatures should already be increasing by approximately half-a-degree Fahrenheit each decade, and should reach 4°F by the middle of the 21st century. These estimates, which have been used to great effect by environmentalists, are based on computer simulations of future climate change, or, as they are called in the trade, General Circulation Models. In fact, *every* greenhouse forecast—every dire prediction of dangerous heat waves, droughts, flooding, radically shifting weather patterns, and the like—is the result of computers attempting to model the myriad factors that influence climate change.

As the IPCC report notes in its summary, "We have substantial confidence that models can predict at least the broad-scale features of climate change." Actually, however, the body of the report, which was written and reviewed by climate scientists, raises all kinds of doubts about the models' reliability. Climate modeling is a difficult and expensive proposition, and modelers themselves are the last to claim that their computers give them much predictive power.

And for good reason. The General Circulation Models attempt to mimic our climate system by using a mathematical simulation of the earth and its oceans and atmosphere. Unfortunately, the mechanisms of our climate are extremely complicated. Take cloud cover, one of the most obvious factors in climate change. Clouds create a problem for the greenhouse models because their influence far outweighs any possible effect of man-made emissions. It is nearly impossible to predict what kinds of clouds will form, or even whether they will serve to enhance or diminish global warming. Depending on your assumptions, you can have the model arrive at pretty much whatever answer you want.

Poor Performance

To gain an idea of how reliable models are, consider how poorly they predict climate changes we have *already* experienced. And if they are incapable of accounting for the past, how will they be able to predict the future?

Over the last 100 years, greenhouse gases in the atmosphere increased by the equivalent of a 50-percent rise in CO_2. Given this increase, the models used by the IPCC would predict a warming of about two degrees over the same 100-year period. But as we have seen, temperatures have increased by only about half that amount—meaning the models have already exaggerated the greenhouse effect by a factor of two.

Reprinted by permission of Chuck Asay and Creators Syndicate.

Even more striking, most of the one-degree warming observed over the last century took place before 1940, while most man-made greenhouse emissions entered the atmosphere *after* 1940. How are greenhouse gases to account for a temperature rise that occurred before they existed?

It gets worse. According to IPCC estimates, the increasing amount of greenhouse gases in the atmosphere should have driven global temperatures up by half a degree in the 1980's alone. Yet satellite measurements of global temperatures, which are the most accurate known, show no significant warming in the 1980's. Where the IPCC's models predicted half a degree, the satellites tell us there was an increase of less than one-tenth of a degree—meaning the models exaggerated by at least a factor of five.

There are other problems with the General Circulation Models. In addition to forecasting a general warming of the earth, the computer simulations predict the specific types of warming that should occur. For example, the Northern Hemisphere should warm more than the Southern, higher latitudes more than lower, and arctic regions most of all. These distinctive characteristics make up the so-called "greenhouse signal." If these changes had actually occurred, it would be a sign that the warming observed over the last 100 years had indeed been caused by man-made carbon emissions.

But no greenhouse signal has been found. There has been no significant difference in temperature trends between the two hemispheres, or between the high and low latitudes, and no significant warming in the arctic.

A Political Issue

In a review of the debate over global warming, Richard Lindzen, Sloan Professor of Meteorology at MIT [Massachusetts Institute of Technology], noted that up until the 1980's, predictions based on computer models "were considered interesting, but largely academic, exercises—even by the scientists involved." What changed in the 1980's was that climate became a political issue. One of the first indications was a 1983 Environmental Protection Agency (EPA) press release claiming that dangerous global warming would occur sometime within the decade, causing sea levels to rise and several coastal cities to go under water. Environmental groups picked up the theme and added it to their already robust list of impending ecological disasters.

Something else changed as well. It is highly unlikely that the scare talk of environmentalists would have made the headway it did among politicians and the general public without the support of leading scientists. By the late 80's, that support was forthcoming.

It was in the stifling summer of 1988 that the greenhouse effect was, as the *Washington Post* put it, "propelled from the scientific journals to the nightly news." On June 23, with the thermometer hitting 98° in Washington, D.C., James Hansen, chief of NASA's Goddard Institute, and a well-known climate expert, announced before a Senate committee that "the greenhouse effect has been detected and it is changing our climate now. . . ." Even more significantly, Hansen said he was "99-percent confident" that current temperatures represent a "real warming trend" rather than natural climate variability.

Hansen's testimony had the effect he must have intended. "We have only one planet," declared the Senate committee chairman, J. Bennett Johnston. "If we screw it up, we have no place to go. The greenhouse effect has ripened beyond theory." Senator Dale Bumpers, sounding a populist note—"What you have is all the economic interests pitted against our very survival"—thought that Hansen's testimony "ought to be a cause for headlines in every newspaper of the country." And so it was. As Stephen Schneider, a climatologist and a major advocate of policies to halt global warming, summed up the reaction to Hansen's report: "Journalists loved it. Environmentalists were ecstatic."

Hansen's testimony, spectacular as it was, constituted only one of a series of endorsements offered by members of the scientific elite to the global-warming scenario. Perhaps the most dramatic was a January 1991 statement sponsored by the Union of Concerned Scientists (UCS) and signed by 700 members of the National Academy of Sciences and over 50 Nobel laureates. There, the UCS warned that burning fossil fuels could cause global temperatures to rise by some 9°F [sic] over the next 100 years. "This process," said the scientists, "could have catastrophic consequences for climate, agriculture, plant and animal species, and coastlines worldwide." Global warming, the statement concluded, was "the most serious environmental threat of the 21st century."

Credible Scientists Question Global Warming

In the face of statements like this, it is no wonder that politicians should take it as established fact that "the greenhouse effect is here" (to quote Hansen again), or should conclude, as then-Senator Timothy Wirth did in 1990, that there were no credible scientists who questioned global warming. But that was most assuredly not the case. In response to Senator Wirth's statement, the late columnist Warren Brookes compiled and published a list of 50 peer-reviewed articles, well-known in the scientific community, which contradicted various parts of the global-warming theory. Moreover, as Richard Lindzen has noted, only a few of those who signed the UCS statement were climate specialists, and after the appeal was released, the president of the National Academy of Sciences warned his colleagues against speaking on subjects about which they could claim no special knowledge.

Environmentalists, of course, have hardly been deterred by

this. Backed, as they assert, by the scientific establishment, they have tended to show open irritation at any attempt to question the threat they have proclaimed. Vice President Al Gore simply dismisses disagreement as bickering that gets in the way of what needs to be done. Others may admit there are doubts, but say we need to act anyway, as an insurance policy. "Uncertainty is no excuse for complacency," argues the UCS.

Here too, as it happens, they are mistaken. According to Michael Schlesinger of the University of Illinois, even if the worst global-warming scenarios were true—which they emphatically are not—delaying a response for five years to wait for more research would cost only one-tenth of a degree of additional warming, so negligible as to be lost in the natural fluctuations of global climate.

"The so-called greenhouse effect could drive global temperatures up as much as 6°F by the year 2100."

The Magnitude of Global Warming May Become Extreme

Michael D. Lemonick

In the following viewpoint, Michael D. Lemonick presents findings released in a 1995 report by the International Panel on Climate Change (IPCC), a United Nations–sponsored organization that conducts research on global warming. According to Lemonick, the IPCC predicts that Earth's atmospheric temperature could increase by as much as 6°Fahrenheit by the year 2100. This rise in temperature would result in disastrous climate changes, Lemonick maintains, including floods and droughts. Lemonick is a senior writer for *Time* magazine.

As you read, consider the following questions:

1. How much has Earth's atmosphere warmed during the past 100 years, according to Lemonick?
2. According to the author, why are computer models more reliable now than they were in the past?
3. How much could sea levels rise during the next 100 years, according to the IPCC, as cited by Lemonick?

Like street-corner prophets proclaiming that the end is near, scientists who study the earth's atmosphere have been issuing predictions of impending doom for the past few years without offering any concrete proof. The atmospheric scientists' version of the apocalypse is global warming, a gradual rise in world-wide temperatures caused by man-made gases trapping too much heat from the sun. If the theory is correct, the world could be in for dramatic changes in climate, accompanied by major disruptions to modern society. So far, though, even the experts have had to admit that while the earth has warmed an average of up to 1.1°F over the past 100 years, no solid evidence has emerged that this is anything but a natural phenomenon. And the uncertainty has given skeptics . . . plenty of ammunition to argue against taking the difficult, expensive steps required to stave off a largely hypothetical calamity.

Until now. A draft report currently circulating on the Internet asserts that the global-temperature rise can now be blamed, at least in part, on human activity. Statements like this have been made before by individual researchers—who have been criticized for going too far beyond the scientific consensus. But this report comes from the International Panel on Climate Change (IPCC), a respected U.N.-sponsored body made up of more than 1,500 leading climate experts from 60 nations.

Unless the world takes immediate and drastic steps to reduce the emissions of heat-trapping gases, says the panel, the so-called greenhouse effect could drive global temperatures up as much as 6°F by the year 2100—an increase in heat comparable to the warming that ended the last Ice Age and with perhaps equally profound effects on climate. Huge swaths of densely populated land could be inundated by rising seas. Entire ecosystems could vanish as rainfall and temperature patterns shift. Droughts, floods and storms could become more severe. Says Michael Oppenheimer, a senior scientist with the Environmental Defense Fund: "I think this is a watershed moment in the public debate on global warming."

This shift in scientific consensus is based not so much on new data as on improvements in the complex computer models that climatologists use to test their theories. Unlike chemists or molecular biologists, climate experts have no way to do lab experiments on their specialty. So they simulate them on supercomputers and look at what happens when human-generated gases—carbon dioxide from industry and auto exhaust, methane from agriculture, chlorofluorocarbons from leaky refrigerators and spray cans—are pumped into the models' virtual atmospheres.

Until recently, the computer models weren't working very well. When the scientists tried to simulate what they believe has been happening over the past century or so, the results didn't mesh with reality; the models said the world should now be warmer than it actually is. The reason is that the computer models had been overlooking an important factor affecting global temperatures: aerosols, the tiny droplets of chemicals like sulfur dioxide that are produced along with CO_2 when fossil fuels are burned in cars and power plants. Aerosols actually cool the planet by blocking sunlight and mask the effects of global warming. Says Tom Wigley, a climatologist at the National Center for Atmospheric Research and a member of the international panel: "We were looking for the needle in the wrong haystack."

A Defense of Computer Models

Critics of global warming say that the computer models cannot be trusted because they fail to reproduce the exact pattern of warming actually experienced over the last century. . . .

Defenders of the models counter that with an extra refinement—taking into account the fact that industrially emitted sulfate aerosols reflect sunlight—the models' forecasts match the historical record much better. . . .

The models appeared to gain some important empirical support in December 1992 when Martin I. Hoffert of New York University and Curt Covey of Lawrence Livermore National Laboratory reconstructed two ancient climates, one much warmer than today's and one much colder. Since they were able to estimate temperature changes and prevailing carbon dioxide levels from evidence in the geological record, they were then in a position to answer the critical question—at least for those two periods—of how much warming is produced by a given rise in carbon dioxide levels.

Their answer was that when carbon dioxide levels double, the temperature of the atmosphere rises by about 4 degrees. This figure agrees well with the best estimate from the computer models, which . . . is that a doubling of carbon dioxide induces a 4.5-degree rise in average global temperature.

William K. Stevens, *New York Times*, September 14, 1993.

Once the scientists factored in aerosols, their models began looking more like the real world. The improved performance of the simulations was demonstrated in 1991, when they successfully predicted temperature changes in the aftermath of the massive Mount Pinatubo eruption in the Philippines. A number of studies since have added to the scientists' confidence that they finally know what they're talking about—and can predict what may happen if greenhouse gases continue to be released into the atmosphere unchecked. Just last week, a report appeared in *Nature* that firmly ties an increase in the severity of U.S. rainstorms to global warming.

In general, the news is not good. Over the next century, says the IPCC report:

• Sea levels could rise up to 3 ft., mostly because of melting glaciers and the expansion of water as it warms up. That could submerge vast areas of low-lying coastal land, including major river deltas, most of the beaches on the U.S. Atlantic Coast, parts of China and the island nations of the Maldives, the Seychelles and the Cook and Marshall islands. More than 100 million people would be displaced.

• Winters could get warmer—which wouldn't bother most people—and warm-weather hot spells like the one that killed 500 in Chicago this past summer could become more frequent and more severe.

• Rainfall could increase overall—but the increase wouldn't be uniform across the globe. Thus areas that are already prone to flooding might flood more often and more severely, and since water evaporates more easily in a warmer world, drought-prone regions and deserts could become even dryer. Hurricanes, which draw their energy from warm oceans, could become even stronger as those oceans heat up.

• Temperature and rainfall patterns would shift in unpredictable ways. That might not pose a problem for agriculture, since farmers could change their crops and irrigate. Natural ecosystems that have to adapt on their own, however, could be devastated. Observes Oppenheimer dryly: "They cannot sprout legs and move to another climate." Perhaps a third of the world's forests, he says, might find themselves living in the wrong places.

These are all worst-case scenarios, and the report's authors acknowledge that plenty of uncertainties remain in their analysis. For example, as the world warms up, it should get cloudier; depending on what sort of clouds predominate, their shadows could offset the warming effect. And nobody knows how the deep ocean currents—which play a major but still murky role in world climate, channeling heat from one part of the globe to another—would respond to global warming.

Some researchers argue that even with these caveats the report overstates the case. Says Richard Lindzen, an atmospheric scientist at M.I.T. [Massachusetts Institute of Technology]: "The margin of error in these models is a factor of 10 or more larger than the effect you're looking for."

Even if Lindzen is wrong and the IPCC report is right, there might not be much anyone could do. Slashing emissions of greenhouse gases to stave off global warming would be straightforward enough, but that doesn't mean it would be easy. Among the strategies recommended in the new report: switching from coal and oil to natural gas, turning to nuclear and solar energy, slowing deforestation, altering land-use and traffic patterns, curbing automobile use, changing life-styles and employment patterns.

In other words, people in the developed world would have to completely transform their society, and rich countries like the U.S. would have to subsidize poor but fast-developing nations like China. And that's just to roll CO_2 emissions back to 1990 levels, the goal most environmentalists endorse. To stave off global warming completely, Lindzen maintains, "you would have to reduce emissions to where they were in 1920." Despite noble proclamations issuing from meetings like the 1992 Earth Summit in Rio, that is virtually inconceivable. As economist Henry Jacoby of M.I.T.'s Sloan School of Management puts it, "If you said, 'Let's design a problem that human institutions can't deal with,' you couldn't find one better than global warming."

> "The analysis . . . leads to 1.1 degrees C as our best estimate for the temperature increase in the next century."

The Magnitude of Global Warming Will Not Be Extreme

Robert Jastrow

In the following viewpoint, Robert Jastrow disputes predictions that global warming will occur at dramatic levels in the twenty-first century. He estimates that if greenhouse gases increase by 100 percent over the next 100 years, as is commonly predicted, Earth's atmosphere will become warmer only by 1.1° Celsius. This rise in temperature, he maintains, would be consistent with natural variations and would not create significant changes in the environment. Jastrow is the president of the George C. Marshall Institute, a public policy research group that specializes in the issue of global warming.

As you read, consider the following questions:

1. According to Jastrow, why did he and his colleagues counsel caution in response to early warnings about global warming?
2. Most of the temperature increase of the past 100 years occurred prior to what year, according to Jastrow?
3. According to the author, what does satellite information reveal about global warming in the 1980s?

Excerpted from Robert Jastrow, "What Happened to the Greenhouse Effect?" *Heritage Lecture #415*, 1992. Reprinted by permission of The Heritage Foundation, © 1992.

A few years ago, I and my colleagues on the board of the George C. Marshall Institute, Bill Nierenberg and Fred Seitz, decided to take a look at the greenhouse effect, because it fitted into the general category of technical issues with a public policy impact. Bill Nierenberg had chaired the first major National Academy of Sciences study on the greenhouse problem, which came out in the 1980s. I had worked in this area when I was last doing active research in NASA at the Goddard Institute for Space Studies. In fact, I had gotten Jim Hansen, who since has become very active in the field, started on the problem when we were looking around for something terrestrial that would bring in some bread-and-butter funding after Jim had been doing his calculations on the atmosphere of Venus.

The fact which triggered our interest in the analysis at that particular time is that the global average temperature has increased simultaneously with an increase in carbon dioxide and other greenhouse gases in the last 100 years. The suggestive correlation in the timing of the increases leads to the tentative conclusion that a global warming produced by the CO_2 increase may have been responsible for some of the warming in the last 100 years, and therefore, will be responsible for more warming in the next 100 years.

The increase in greenhouse gases is equivalent to about a 50 percent increase in CO_2, relative to the 19th century. Half of that is CO_2 itself and the other half is the equivalent in warming effect from other greenhouse gases like methane. The projections of energy growth into the 21st century suggest an increase of 100 percent in CO_2 equivalent over today's level, between now and roughly the mid-21st century. Recent revisions tend to push that doubling off to the end of the 21st century, but in any case, it is projected that some time in the next century the greenhouse gases will double and their warming effect will be correspondingly increased.

Counselling Caution

We looked into this matter, and being familiar with the computer models that are used to forecast climate in the next century, we counselled caution. As you may know, these models have some defects; one predicts, for example, equal amounts of rain in Scotland and in the Sahara Desert. So, they have to be used with caution, and we thought a few more years of study would give us better information.

But we also noticed something peculiar in our initial look at the temperature data, and that appears in Chart 1.

This shows the measured values of average global temperature, as best you can fit together a global picture from a mixture of land stations plus a very sparse coverage over the oceans and the poles. The global average of the temperature measurements shows an increase of about a half a degree Celsius in the last hundred years. The calculations of rising temperature caused by the greenhouse effect—the one in the chart is taken from a paper by Jim Hansen—also show an increase of about half a degree in the last hundred years. That agreement seemed significant, and Dr. Hansen mentioned in congressional testimony in 1988 that he was pretty certain there was a connection between these two increases. He said in June 1988, "Global warming is now sufficiently large that we can ascribe with a high degree of confidence a cause-and-effect relationship to the greenhouse effect."

What we noticed that seemed peculiar was that nearly all of the temperature increase occurred prior to 1940; from 1940 to

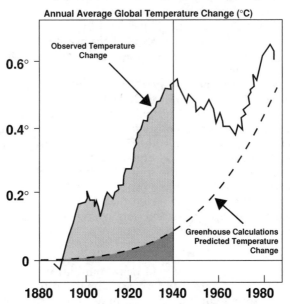

Chart 1. Greenhouse Calculations Fail to Explain Global Temperature Changes

Annual Average Global Temperature Change (°C)

Note: Both greenhouse calculations and observed global temperatures of the last 100 years show a rise of about 0.5°C. However, most of the observed rise occurred before 1940, while most of the greenhouse gases entered the atmosphere after 1940. The greenhouse gases cannot be the cause of a temperature rise that occurred before the gases existed. The lightly shaded area shows the observed temperature rise. The heavily shaded area shows the small part of the rise that can be attributed to the greenhouse effect.

Source: The George C. Marshall Institute, *Global Warming Update*, 1992.

the present, the temperature moved up and down, but there has been little net change. However, most of the greenhouse gases—two-thirds to be precise—came into the atmosphere *after* 1940. Greenhouse gases cannot produce a warming that occurred before they existed, so the correlation between the two half-degree increases becomes suspect. This would seem to indicate conclusively that other factors are influencing climate besides, or in addition to, the greenhouse effect.

A Lower Estimate

In the second Marshall report, we focused on setting a limit to the magnitude of the greenhouse warming, using the currently available data. We used the measured response of the earth to the 50 percent increase in greenhouse gases to date, as a way of calibrating what the earth would be doing in the next century, when these gases increase by another 100 percent over today's levels.

As I noted, a 50 percent increase in CO_2 and other greenhouse gases has produced roughly half a degree Celsius of warming. Actually, the greenhouse gases could not have produced that entire half-degree of warming. But for the purpose of deriving an upper limit on the magnitude of the greenhouse effect in the next century, we chose to attribute all the half-degree warming that has occurred to date to greenhouse gases, even though we knew that is not correct and at least part of the half-degree increase must be due to some other cause.

So, we assumed that a half-degree is the response of the earth—the real earth, with all the complicated cloud feedbacks and ocean feedbacks accurately entered, because this is the planet itself and not a computer model—to a 50 percent increase in CO_2. Now, for small temperature changes like this, and allowing for the roughly logarithmic dependence on the CO_2 concentration, if a 50 percent increase produces half a degree Celsius (C) of warming, then the 100 percent increase projected for the mid-21st century will produce roughly an additional one degree C of warming.

Doing the analysis in greater detail, with allowance for the so-called natural variability of climate as well as the uncertainty in the temperature observations, leads to 1.1 degrees C as our best estimate for the temperature increase in the next century. This result is to be compared with a "best estimate" of 2.5 degrees C put forward as the consensus of the computer models by the United Nations Intergovernmental Panel on Climate Change, or IPCC. So, our estimate for an upper limit on the mid-21st century warming is somewhat lower than the mid-range "best estimate" of the U.N. committee.

The Marshall Institute released a report including these results in 1991. Our Board took another look at the situation in

1992, by way of incorporating new evidence that has come to light in the interim. The more recent Marshall findings are incorporated in a third report called "Global Warming Update." The principal information that led us to look at the matter again is the record of thirteen years of accurate satellite measurements of global temperature. These satellite measurements are shown in Chart 2.

Chart 2. Global Warming? Satellites Show Minimal Temperature Increase Over Last Decade

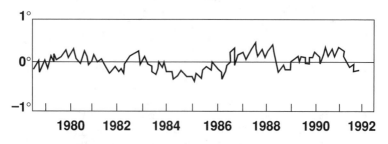

Note: Satellite measurements of global temperature do not show the large expected upwards trend due to the greenhouse effect. Increases in some years are balanced by decreases in others. The average increase in the data is 0.06°C/decade. The 1992 Scientific Assessment report of the IPCC gives 0.3°C/decade as the consensus of theoretical predictions for the temperature increase due to the greenhouse gases—five times greater than the effect revealed by the satellite measurements.

Source: The George C. Marshall Institute, *Global Warming Update*, 1992.

They are interesting because they give a fairly uniform sampling over the oceans and the polar areas, and not only the continents. A check against measurements made on the ground shows that these satellite measurements reflect very accurately the actual temperature values on the surface of the earth. Scientists who disagree with the implication in the satellite measurements say the satellite data are subject to uncertainties because they measure the atmosphere rather than the ground. But the correlation between the ground measurements and the satellite measurements for the entire North American continent—a respectably large piece of real estate—is 0.98. Now, 1.00 is perfect correlation; that is how data correlate with themselves. A correlation of 0.98 is about as good as you can get for the agreement between two independently measured sets of data. It indicates that these are very reliable measures of ground temperature. In fact, they probably give a better global picture than the so-called global averages of the surface data, which must rely on very sparse ocean and high-latitude coverage.

Now to the point: The satellite measurements show essentially no trend in the 1980s. The IPCC report quotes the consensus of the various computer models of climate change as predicting a greenhouse warming in the 1980s of about 0.3 degrees C per decade. That would be about 0.4 degrees C for the thirteen-year period shown here. The trend line through the satellite data yields 0.06 degrees per decade. This is one-fifth of the warming of 0.3 degrees C per decade which is the consensus of the computer models.

Once again, we have used the real earth, and its actual temperature changes, to calibrate the reaction of the earth's climate to an increase in greenhouse gases, and we find an answer which is one-fifth as large as the consensus of the computer models. So, if the IPCC gives the "best estimate" of the computer models as 2.5 degrees C for the mid-21st century, we suggest that this value should be cut by a factor of five to 0.5 degrees C. A rise of 0.5 degrees C should be the result of a 100 percent increase in CO_2. This result is consistent with the upper limit of 1.1 degrees C for a doubling of CO_2, which was reported in the previous Marshall analysis.

Based on satellite measurements which give the earth's real response to the real increase that has occurred to date, and not on theoretical models, this is the firmest evidence we have thus far on the magnitude of global warming to be expected in the next century.

A half-degree rise, spread over the better part of a century, would not be noticeable against the natural background of temperature variations. It would not justify carbon taxes or any other kind of restriction on energy production and the burning of fossil fuels.

41

"*More scientists are becoming openly skeptical about . . . predictions of a major global warming in the twenty-first century.*"

The Theory of Global Warming Is Not Scientifically Credible

S. Fred Singer

S. Fred Singer is professor emeritus of environmental studies at the University of Virginia and the director of the Science and Environmental Policy Project in Washington, D.C. In the following viewpoint, Singer contends that the theory of global warming is not a scientifically sound concept. He argues that the computer models used to predict global temperature increases resulting from atmospheric greenhouse gases are unreliable. According to Singer, attempts to use these models to reproduce current climate trends have failed, thus proving that the models are invalid for predicting future temperature changes.

As you read, consider the following questions:

1. In what ways do researchers manipulate their computer models, according to Singer?
2. According to the author, what per decade global temperature change is predicted by the Intergovernmental Panel on Climate Change's *Policymakers Summary*? How does this estimate compare to the estimate made by John Christy?

S. Fred Singer, "Chilling Out on Warming," *Washington Times*, October 11, 1994, p. A14. Reprinted by permission of the author.

The science basis for climate warming is coming under attack in the world's leading scientific journals, just as the U.N.-sponsored Intergovernmental Panel on Climate Change [makes] scary predictions of future climate disasters.

While the IPCC leaders and activists call for ever deeper cuts in the emission of carbon dioxide from the burning of fuels, by further constraining the use of energy, a September 22, 1994, editorial in *Nature* chastises them for supporting such far-reaching recommendations with little more than press releases and executive summaries, describing them as a "euphemism for sound-bites directed at those who do not read." The editorial also notes that "argument persists in the scientific community about the effects [of CO_2] on climate."

Primitive "Models"

Nature is right on the mark. There is not, nor ever was a "scientific consensus" in support of climate catastrophes—as so often claimed by political types. Scientists recognize that climate forecasts are simply the result of still quite primitive "models" of the real atmosphere fed into giant computers. Basically skeptics, they ask: How trustworthy are these models?

There is no observable evidence as yet that global warming is taking place—despite the continuing increase in the atmospheric concentration of CO_2 and other greenhouse gases. Ground stations and satellite instruments have not documented the expected temperature rise of 1 to 2 degrees C. As time passes and negative data accumulate, more scientists are becoming openly skeptical about the IPCC predictions of a major global warming in the twenty-first century.

Worse still for the professional doom-merchants: The models don't even agree with each other; their forecasts depend on the detailed way in which they are set up. This important fact has been known for a long time among scientific specialists; but now at last the public has been let in on the secret. In the September 9, 1994, issue of *Science*, reporter Richard Kerr reveals the "fudging" that modelers engage in to make the models come up with the correct numbers.

For a model to predict future climate with any credibility, it must first be able to reproduce the *current* climate. But to do this, Mr. Kerr reports, "nearly everybody cheats a little." In other words, modelers are forced to manipulate their models to make them agree with today's climate. Some do this by "adjusting" the transfer of energy between ocean and atmosphere. Others "tune" their models by changing the strength of the solar radiation until they get just the right answer. If garbage goes into models, can what comes out be anything but garbage?

Now, a research group at the Massachusetts Institute of Technology, headed by Professor Peter Stone, has conducted a computer experiment to test whether such artificially fixed models are reliable. Their result pretty well lays to rest any notion that current greenhouse models can be used as a basis for policy—for the Global Climate Treaty [adopted at the 1992 Earth Summit in Rio de Janeiro] or for any of the frantic efforts to control emissions.

The MIT group deliberately put an error into their model so that too much moisture was transported through the atmosphere. When projected into a future with higher atmospheric CO_2, the model predicted weakened Atlantic Ocean currents, with dire consequences for world climate. They then adjusted the model until they got the correct current climate, thus covering up the error. Not surprisingly, however, the predictions did not get any better, demonstrating anew that "tuning" does not overcome any basic errors inherent in the model.

Of course, none of this will ever make the front page. Environmental activists, politicians and bureaucrats will continue on their merry way . . . trying to curtail the use of energy, impose huge financial burdens on consumers, and upset national economies—all in utter disregard of the underlying science. They might enlighten themselves by reading in full the widely touted *IPCC Report on Climate Change*, written by some 300 scientists and published by Cambridge University Press in 1990, rather than simply relying on the misleading *Policymakers Summary*, prepared by a handful of IPCC editors.

Scientific Findings

Here is what they would find (emphasis added):

• W.L. Gates (chief modeler at the Livermore National Laboratory in California), P.R. Rowntree and Q.C. Zheng, in the 1990 IPCC report, Section 4, "Validation of Climate Models":

"[Climate models] display a number of systematic errors in common. . . . These model errors and sensitivities, and our current uncertainty over how best to represent the process involved, require a serious consideration of the extent to which we can have confidence in the performance of models on different scales." (page 99.)

"The existence of such common deficiencies, despite the considerable differences in the models' resolution, numerical treatments and physical parameterizations, implies that all models may be misrepresenting (or indeed omitting) some physical mechanisms." (page 102.)

• G. McBean (head of the Canadian Weather Service) and J.M. McCarthy (Harvard University), in the IPCC report, Section 11, "Narrowing the Uncertainties":

"Present [model] shortcomings include: Significant uncertainty, by a range of three, regarding the sensitivity of the global average temperature and mean sea-level to the increase in greenhouse gases; Even larger uncertainties regarding regional climatic impacts, such that current climate change predictions have little meaning for any particular location." (page 317.)

"If the atmosphere and upper-ocean alone were responding to the increase in greenhouse heating and the cloud-radiation feedback operated according to current knowledge, then the surface of the Earth would already be *1 to 2 degrees C warmer* than the temperatures of the 19th century." (page 321.)

Compare these numbers with the farfetched claim in the IPCC *Policymakers Summary*, page xii: "Global mean surface air temperature has increased by *0.3 to 0.6°C* over the last 100 years . . . *broadly consistent* with predictions of climate models."

A Tool with Limited Use

Scientific controversy over "global warming" continues. . . .

One area of controversy has to do with the reliability of computer models of the global climate system. Can they accurately predict future climate change?

At this point, the answer is no. . . .

Computer simulations of the climate, referred to as "general circulation models" (GCMs), can be used to assess the sensitivity of climate to changes that might result from increased greenhouse gases. However, because physical feedbacks between Earth's atmosphere (including clouds), the ocean, and the biosphere remain incomplete in the models, their use as a tool is limited.

Roger Pielke, *Christian Science Monitor*, August 24, 1994.

• From the 1990 *Policymakers Summary*, page xi: "Based on current model results, we predict . . . a rate of increase of global mean temperature . . . of about *0.3°C per decade*." Compare this predicted positive trend with the observed negative trend in Professor John Christy's report of the highly accurate satellite data (September 9, 1994): "Decadal global trend since 1979 [for the lower troposphere] is ⁻0.064 degrees C."

• Dr. Bruce Callander, current head of the IPCC Science Panel, was quoted in London's *Financial Times* (March 18, 1994, page 14): "Cloud behavior is the 'single biggest uncertainty.' Researchers cannot be certain whether [clouds] speed warming or slow it . . . in 10 years we may say [scientists' investigation] has been *an interesting exercise which came to nothing*, or we may say that we were recognizing something important happening in the atmosphere."

Responsible scientists have tried to convey their concern for some time. The late Professor Roger Revelle, universally acknowledged as having called attention to enhanced greenhouse warming, wrote to Representative Jim Bates on July 18, 1988:

"Most scientists familiar with the subject are not yet willing to bet that the climate this year is the result of 'greenhouse warming.' As you very well know, climate is highly variable from year to year, and the causes of these variations are not at all well understood. My own personal belief is that we should *wait another 10 or 20 years* to really be convinced that the greenhouse is going to be important for human beings, in *both positive and negative ways*."

On July 18 of that year, Mr. Revelle wrote a similar letter to then-Senator Tim Wirth, now undersecretary of state for everything global.

It was good advice then. It's good advice now, as the accumulating scientific evidence makes the reality of a major warming less likely.

"The energy industry has been conducting . . . a ferocious public relations campaign meant to sell the notion that science . . . is always a matter of uncertainty."

The Theory of Global Warming Is Scientifically Credible

Ross Gelbspan

Many scientists and public policy experts criticize the scientific theories and methods on which predictions of global warming are based. In the following viewpoint, Ross Gelbspan maintains that these attacks on the scientific credibility of global warming are part of a deceptive public relations campaign funded by oil and energy corporations. Gelbspan insists that the threat of global warming has been substantiated by numerous scientific findings. Gelbspan is a retired newspaper editor and reporter who wrote extensively about environmental issues during his career.

As you read, consider the following questions:

1. What geophysical events suggest that global warming is a serious problem, in Gelbspan's view?
2. According to the author, how much money did the Global Climate Coalition spend between 1993 and 1995 to downplay the threat of climate change?
3. From whom has S. Fred Singer received consulting fees, according to Gelbspan?

The reports of changes in the world's climate have been with us for fifteen or twenty years, most urgently since 1988, when Dr. James Hansen, director of NASA's Goddard Institute for Space Studies, declared that the era of global warming was at hand. As a newspaper correspondent who had reported on the United Nations Conferences on the environment in Stockholm in 1972 and in Rio in 1992, I understood something of the ill effects apt to result from the extravagant burning of oil and coal. New record-setting weather extremes seem to have become as commonplace as traffic accidents, and three simple facts have long been known: the distance from the surface of the earth to the far edge of the inner atmosphere is only twelve miles; the annual amount of carbon dioxide forced into that limited space is six billion tons; and the ten hottest years in recorded human history have all occurred since 1980. The facts beg a question that is as simple to ask as it is hard to answer. What do we do with what we know?

An Unambiguous Conclusion

The question became more pointed in September 1995, when the 2,500 climate scientists serving on the Intergovernmental Panel on Climate Change issued a new statement on the prospect of forthcoming catastrophe. Never before had the IPCC (called into existence in 1988) come to so unambiguous a conclusion. Always in years past there had been people saying that we didn't yet know enough, or that the evidence was problematical, or our system of computer simulation was subject to too many uncertainties. Not this year. The panel flatly announced that the earth had entered a period of climatic instability likely to cause "widespread economic, social and environmental dislocation over the next century." The continuing emission of greenhouse gases would create protracted, crop-destroying droughts in continental interiors, a host of new and recurring diseases, hurricanes of extraordinary malevolence, and rising sea levels that could inundate island nations and low-lying coastal rims on the continents.

I came across the report in the *New York Times* during the same week that the island of St. Thomas was blasted to shambles by one of thirteen hurricanes that roiled the Caribbean that fall. Scientists speak the language of probability. They prefer to avoid making statements that cannot be further corrected, reinterpreted, modified, or proven wrong. If its September announcement was uncharacteristically bold, possibly it was because the IPCC scientists understood that they were addressing their remarks to people profoundly unwilling to hear what they had to say.

That resistance is understandable, given the immensity of the stakes. The energy industries now constitute the largest single

48

enterprise known to mankind. Moreover, they are indivisible from automobile, farming, shipping, air freight, and banking interests, as well as from the governments dependent on oil revenues for their very existence. With annual sales in excess of one trillion dollars and daily sales of more than two billion dollars, the oil industry alone supports the economies of the Middle East and large segments of the economies of Russia, Mexico, Venezuela, Nigeria, Indonesia, Norway, and Great Britain. Begin to enforce restriction on the consumption of oil and coal, and the effects on the global economy—unemployment, depression, social breakdown, and war—might lay waste to what we have come to call civilization. It is no wonder that since the early 1990s many of the world's politicians and most of the world's news media have been promoting the perception that the worries about the weather are overwrought. Ever since the IPCC first set out to devise strategies whereby the nations of the world might reduce their carbon dioxide emissions, and thus ward off a rise in the average global temperature on the order of 4 or 5 degrees Celsius (roughly equal in magnitude to the difference between the last ice age and the current climatic period), the energy industry has been conducting, not unreasonably, a ferocious public relations campaign meant to sell the notion that science, any science, is always a matter of uncertainty. Yet on reading the news from the IPCC, I wondered how the oil company publicists would confront the most recent series of geophysical events and scientific findings. To wit:

• A 48-by-22-mile chunk of the Larsen Ice Shelf in the Antarctic broke off in March 1995, exposing rocks that had been buried for 20,000 years and prompting Rodolfo del Valle of the Argentine Antarctic Institute to tell the Associated Press, "Last November we predicted the [ice shelf] would crack in ten years, but it has happened in barely two months."

• In April 1995, researchers discovered a 70 percent decline in the population of zooplankton off the coast of southern California, raising questions about the survival of several species of fish that feed on it. Scientists have linked the change to a 1 to 2 degree C increase in the surface water temperature over the last four decades.

• A recent series of articles in the *Lancet*, a British medical journal, linked changes in climate patterns to the spread of infectious diseases around the world. The *Aedes aegypti* mosquito, which spreads dengue fever and yellow fever, has traditionally been unable to survive at altitudes higher than 1,000 meters above sea level. But these mosquitoes are now being reported at 1,150 meters in Costa Rica and at 2,200 meters in Colombia. Ocean warming has triggered algae blooms linked to outbreaks of cholera in India, Bangladesh, and the Pacific coast of South America, where, in 1991, the disease infected more than 400,000 people.

• In a paper published in *Science* in April 1995, David J. Thomson, of the AT&T Bell Laboratories, concluded that the .6 degree C warming of the average global temperature over the past century correlates directly with the buildup of atmospheric carbon dioxide. Separate findings by a team of scientists at the National Oceanic and Atmospheric Administration's National Climatic Data Center indicate that growing weather extremes in the United States are due, by a probability of 90 percent, to rising levels of greenhouse gases.

Toles. Copyright The Buffalo News. Reprinted with permission of Universal Press Syndicate. All rights reserved.

• Scientists previously believed that the transitions between ice ages and more moderate climatic periods occur gradually, over centuries. But researchers from the Woods Hole Oceanographic Institution, examining deep ocean sediment and ice core samples, found that these shifts, with their temperature changes of up to 7 degrees C, have occurred within three to four decades—a virtual nanosecond in geological time. Over the last 70,000 years, the earth's climate has snapped into radically different temperature regimes. "Our results suggest that the present climate system is very delicately poised," said researcher Scott Lehman. "Shifts could happen very rapidly if conditions are right, and we cannot predict when that will occur." His cautionary tone is underscored by findings that the end of the last ice age, some 8,000 years ago, was preceded by a series of extreme oscillations in which severe regional deep freezes alternated with warming spikes. As the North Atlantic warmed, Arctic snowmelts and increased rainfall diluted the salt content of the ocean, which, in turn, redirected the ocean's warming current from a northeasterly direction to one that ran nearly due east. Should such an episode occur today, say researchers, "the present climate of Britain and Norway would change suddenly to that of Greenland."

Intentional Confusion

These items (and many like them) would seem to be alarming news . . . worthy of a national debate or the sustained attention of Congress. But the signs and portents have been largely ignored, relegated to the environmental press and the oddball margins of the mass media. More often than not, the news about the accelerating retreat of the world's glaciers or the heat- and insect-stressed Canadian forests comes qualified with the observation that the question of global warming never can be conclusively resolved. The confusion is intentional, expensively gift wrapped by the energy industries.

Capital keeps its nose to the wind. The people who run the world's oil and coal companies know that the march of science, and of political action, may be slowed by disinformation. Between 1993 and 1995, one of the leading oil industry public relations outlets, the Global Climate Coalition, spent more than a million dollars to downplay the threat of climate change. It expected to spend another $850,000 on the issue in 1996. Similarly, the National Coal Association spent more than $700,000 on the global climate issue in 1992 and 1993. In 1993 alone, the American Petroleum Institute, just one of fifty-four industry members of the GCC, paid $1.8 million to the public relations firm of Burson-Marsteller partly in an effort to defeat a proposed tax on fossil fuels. For perspective, this is only slightly less than the combined yearly expenditures on global warming of the five major environmental groups that focus on climate issues—about $2.1 million, according to officials of the Environmental Defense Fund, the Natural Resources Defense Council, the Sierra Club, the Union of Concerned Scientists, and the World Wildlife Fund.

For the most part the industry has relied on a small band of skeptics—Dr. Richard S. Lindzen, Dr. Pat Michaels, Dr. Robert Balling, Dr. Sherwood Idso, and Dr. S. Fred Singer, among others—who have proven extraordinarily adept at draining the issue of all sense of crisis. Through their frequent pronouncements in the press and on radio and television, they have helped to create the illusion that the question is hopelessly mired in unknowns. Most damaging has been their influence on decision makers; their contrarian views have allowed conservative Republicans such as Representative Dana Rohrabacher (R., Calif.) to dismiss legitimate research concerns as "liberal claptrap" and have provided the basis for . . . budget cuts to those government science programs designed to monitor the health of the planet.

The St. Paul Hearings

In May 1995, Minnesota held hearings in St. Paul to determine the environmental cost of coal burning by state power plants. Three of the skeptics—Lindzen, Michaels, and Balling—were hired as expert witnesses to testify on behalf of Western Fuels Association, a $400 million consortium of coal suppliers and coal-fired utilities.

An especially aggressive industry player, Western Fuels was quite candid about its strategy in two annual reports: "[T]here has been a close to universal impulse in the trade association community here in Washington to concede the scientific premise of global warming . . . while arguing over policy prescriptions that would be the least disruptive to our economy. . . . We have disagreed, and do disagree, with this strategy." "When [the climate change] controversy first erupted . . . scientists were found who are skeptical about much of what seemed generally accepted about the potential for climate change." Among them were Michaels, Balling, and S. Fred Singer.

Lindzen, a distinguished professor of meteorology at MIT [Massachusetts Institute of Technology], testified in St. Paul that the maximum probable warming of the atmosphere in the face of a doubling of carbon dioxide emissions over the next century would amount to no more than a negligible .3 degrees C. Michaels, who teaches climatology at the University of Virginia, stated that he foresaw no increase in the rate of sea level rise—another feared precursor of global warming. Balling, who works on climate issues at Arizona State University, declared that the increase in emissions would boost the average global temperature by no more than one degree.

At first glance, these attacks appear defensible, given their focus on the black holes of uncertainty that mark our current knowledge of the planet's exquisitely interrelated climate system. The skeptics emphasize the inadequacy of a major climate research tool known as a General Circulation Model, and our ignorance of carbon dioxide exchange between the oceans and the atmosphere and of the various roles of clouds. They have repeatedly pointed out that although the world's output of carbon dioxide has exploded since 1940, there has been no corresponding increase in the global temperature. The larger scientific community, by contrast, holds that this is due to the masking effect of low-level sulfur particulates, which exert a temporary cooling effect on the earth, and to a time lag in the oceans' absorption and release of carbon dioxide.

But while the skeptics portray themselves as besieged truthseekers fending off irresponsible environmental doomsayers, their testimony in St. Paul and elsewhere revealed the source and scope of their funding for the first time. Michaels received more than $115,000 between 1991 and 1995 from coal and energy interests. *World Climate Review*, a quarterly he founded that routinely debunks climate concerns, was funded by Western Fuels. Between 1989 and 1995, either alone or with colleagues, Balling has received more than $200,000 from coal and oil interests in Great Britain, Germany, and elsewhere. Balling (along with Sherwood Idso) has also taken money from Cyprus Minerals, a mining company that has been a major funder of People for the West—a militantly anti-environmental "Wise Use" group. Lindzen, for his part, charges oil and coal interests $2,500 a day for his consulting services; his 1991 trip to testify before a Senate committee was paid for by Western Fuels, and a speech he wrote, entitled "Global Warming: the Origin and Nature of Alleged Scientific Consensus," was underwritten by OPEC. Singer, who proposed a $95,000 publicity project to "stem the tide towards ever more onerous controls on energy use," has received consulting fees from Exxon, Shell, Unocal, ARCO, and Sun Oil, and has warned them that they face the same threat as the chemical firms that produced chlorofluorocarbons (CFCs), a class of chemicals found to be depleting atmospheric ozone. "It took only five years to go from . . . a simple freeze of production [of CFCs]," Singer has written, ". . . to the 1992 decision of a complete production phase-out—all on the basis of quite insubstantial science."

The skeptics assert flatly that their science is untainted by funding. Nevertheless, in this persistent and well-funded campaign of denial they have become interchangeable ornaments on the hood of a high-powered engine of disinformation. Their dissenting opinions are amplified beyond all proportion through the media while the concerns of the dominant majority of the world's scientific establishment are marginalized. By keeping the discussion focused on whether there is a problem in the first place, they have effectively silenced the debate over what to do about it.

Periodical Bibliography

The following articles have been selected to supplement the diverse views presented in this chapter. Addresses are provided for periodicals not indexed in the *Readers' Guide to Periodical Literature*, the *Alternative Press Index*, or the *Social Sciences Index*.

AIM Report	"Global Warming—or Media Hot Air?" vol. A, March 1992. Available from 4455 Connecticut Ave. NW, Suite 330, Washington, DC 20008.
Gary Benoit	"Warm Earth, Cold Earth," *New American*, May 1, 1995. Available from PO Box 8040, Appleton, WI 54913.
Robert Bindschadler	"Frozen Peril," *World & I*, April 1995. Available from 3600 New York Ave. NE, Washington, DC 20002.
Hugh W. Ellsaesser	"Climate Reality, Not Politics, Should Determine Policy," *21st Century*, Summer 1995. Available from PO Box 16285, Washington, DC 20041.
Environment	Entire issue on global warming, July/August 1993. Available from 1319 18th St. NW, Washington, DC 20036-1802.
Christopher Flavin	"Storm Warnings," *World Watch*, November/December 1994. Available from PO Box 6991, Syracuse, NY 13217-9942.
Marsha Freeman	"We Are Unable to Answer Even the Most Basic Questions," *21st Century*, Spring 1995.
Tee L. Guidotti	"Global Climate Change and Human Ecology," *PSR Quarterly*, December 1993. Available from 10 Brookline Place W., Brookline, MA 02146.
Paul Harvey	"The New Protection Racket," *Conservative Chronicle*, March 24, 1996. Available from Box 29, Hampton, IA 50441.
Richard S. Lindzen	"Global Warming: The Origin and Nature of the Alleged Scientific Consensus," *Cato Review of Business and Government Regulation*, Spring 1992. Available from 1000 Massachusetts Ave. NW, Washington, DC 20001.
Jeffrey Marsh	"Taking Mother Earth's Temperature," *American Enterprise*, July/August 1993.
Charles T. Rubin and Marc K. Landy	"Global Warming," *Garbage*, February/March 1993.
Jocelyn Tomkin	"Hot Air," *Reason*, March 1993.
Robert Wright	"Some Like It Hot," *New Republic*, October 9, 1995.

2 CHAPTER

What Causes
Global Warming?

GLOBAL
WARMING

Chapter Preface

Most scientists and researchers agree that the greatest contributor to global warming is the increasing amount of carbon dioxide that is released into the atmosphere by natural and human-made causes. But some scientists think that another gas—methane—may play a larger role in global warming than was previously believed.

Methane, or CH_4, is a gas that is formed when organic matter decomposes. The largest producers of methane are landfills, coal mines, termites, livestock, and wetlands such as peat bogs and rice paddies. Like carbon dioxide, methane traps heat energy and reflects it back to the earth's surface, but it does so at twenty to twenty-five times the rate of carbon dioxide. Researchers have discovered that the amount of atmospheric methane doubled during the twentieth century and is increasing at a rate of 1 percent per year, twice the rate of carbon dioxide. This increase in atmospheric methane alarms some scientists, who estimate that methane, at only one-two hundredth the concentration of carbon dioxide, may be responsible for 12 percent of the earth's warming since the mid-1980s.

Yet many scientists believe that the increasing concentrations of methane are merely a consequence—rather than a cause—of global warming. James Kennett, director of the Marine Science Institute at the University of California at Santa Barbara, admits that glacial ice formed during warming periods that occurred thirty-eight thousand and forty-four thousand years ago contains large concentrations of methane, but he asserts that this finding does not prove methane is responsible for global warming. Kennett argues that as carbon dioxide emissions increase, the ocean temperatures rise, melting frozen methane crystals in the ocean floor. The methane released from the frozen crystals bubbles up to the surface and into the atmosphere, Kennett contends, which explains the high concentrations of atmospheric methane found during warming periods in the ice ages. The current trend of increased levels of methane could also be a result of this same process, he maintains.

Methane, sunspots, and carbon dioxide emissions—both natural and human-made—have all been blamed for causing global warming. The authors in the following chapter present various opinions on the reasons for the warming of the earth's atmosphere.

"*Human activity is a likely cause of the warming of the global atmosphere.*"

Human Activity Causes Global Warming

William K. Stevens

Burning wood and fossil fuels such as oil and coal releases carbon dioxide—a greenhouse gas—into the air. According to scientists interviewed by William K. Stevens in the following viewpoint, the burning of these fossil fuels has caused global warming by increasing the amount of greenhouse gases in the Earth's atmosphere. Therefore, the scientists conclude, human activities are primarily responsible for global warming. Stevens is a reporter with the *New York Times*.

As you read, consider the following questions:

1. In the author's view, why did many scientists wait until 1995 to declare that human activities are most likely responsible for global warming?
2. What is the role of the Intergovernmental Panel on Climate Change, according to Stevens?
3. By how much do scientists expect average global temperatures to rise by the year 2100, as cited by Stevens?

In an important shift of scientific judgment, experts advising the world's governments on climate change are saying for the first time that human activity is a likely cause of the warming of the global atmosphere.

While many climatologists have thought this to be the case, all but a few held until late 1995 that the climate is so naturally variable that they could not be sure they were seeing a clear signal of the feared greenhouse effect—the heating of the atmosphere because of the carbon dioxide released by burning coal, oil and wood.

Even the string of very warm years in the 1980's and 1990's could have been just a natural swing of the climatic pendulum, the experts have said.

Data Suggest Human Causes

But a growing body of data and analysis suggests that the warming of the last century, and especially of the last few years, "is unlikely to be entirely due to natural causes and that a pattern of climatic response to human activities is identifiable in the climatological record," says a draft summary of a new report by the Intergovernmental Panel on Climate Change.

The panel's role is to advise governments negotiating reductions in emissions of greenhouse gases like carbon dioxide under the 1992 treaty on climate change.

The panel's draft summary, although intended for internal use, was made available on the Internet. The draft has been through at least one round of scientific review but its wording may change, since it is being reviewed by governments. Scientists who prepared the full chapter on which the summary statement is based say they do not expect any substantial change in their basic assessment. The chapter has gone through extensive review by scientists around the world.

"I think the scientific justification for the statement is there, unequivocally," said Dr. Tom M. L. Wigley, a climatologist at the National Center for Atmospheric Research in Boulder, Colo., one of the chapter's authors.

The scientific community "has discovered the smoking gun," said Dr. Michael Oppenheimer, an atmospheric scientist with the Environmental Defense Fund, who is familiar with the draft report. "This finding is of paramount importance. For many years, policy makers have asked, 'Where's the signal?'" The intergovernmental panel, he said, "is telling us that the signal is here."

But Dr. Wigley and others involved in the reassessment say it is not yet known how much of the last century's warming can be attributed to human activity and how much is part of the earth's natural fluctuation that leads to ice ages at one extreme and warm periods at the other.

Nevertheless, the panel's conclusion marks a watershed in the views of climatologists, who with the notable exception of Dr. James E. Hansen of the NASA Goddard Institute for Space Studies in New York have until 1995 refused to declare publicly that they can discern the signature of the greenhouse effect.

The new consensus, as represented by the intergovernmental panel, seems likely to stimulate more public debate over how seriously the threat of climate change should be taken.

Warming: Seeking a Signal Amid Static

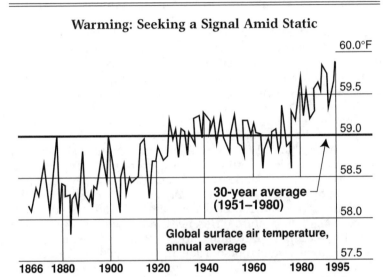

Amid the natural variability of temperature, a growing body of data suggests that the warming of the last century and especially since the late 1980s reflects a pattern of response to human activities.

Source: NASA Goddard Institute for Space Studies.

As for the future, the draft summary forecasts an increase in the average global temperature of 1.44 degrees to 6.3 degrees Fahrenheit by the year 2100 if there is no further action to curb emissions of greenhouse gases. But that represents only 50 to 70 percent of the eventual warming, it says. These changes would be more rapid than any in the last 10,000 years, the period in which civilization developed, the panel says.

And it says that whatever action is taken in the future, the world still faces a further average temperature increase of 1 to 3.6 degrees.

By comparison, according to varying estimates, the average

global temperature is 5 to 9 degrees warmer now than in the last ice age.

While a warmer world could be beneficial in some ways, the draft says, there would be many adverse effects. These include more extreme weather and possibly more intense tropical storms, destruction of some communities by rising seas, damage to and loss of natural ecosystems that cannot adapt rapidly enough, diminished agricultural output in some places and an increase in some tropical diseases.

Experts agree that the average surface temperature of the globe has already risen about 1 degree Fahrenheit in the last century, but there has long been debate over the cause.

Much of the argument has involved the computerized models of the atmosphere that have been climatologists' main tools in analyzing the warming problem. The models have many imperfections, but the panel scientists say they have improved and are being used more effectively.

Scientists say that a major reason for the change in view marked by the new report, in fact, is that a new generation of studies has enhanced their confidence in computer simulations of the atmosphere, creating a much better agreement between predicted patterns of climate change and those actually observed.

One study in particular, led by Dr. Benjamin B. Santer of the Lawrence Livermore National Laboratory, found a good match between the temperature differences from region to region predicted by computerized simulations of the atmosphere's response to increased carbon dioxide and those actually measured.

Dr. Santer is also an author of the intergovernmental panel's chapter on causes of the warming, along with Dr. Wigley, Dr. Tim P. Barnett of the Scripps Institution of Oceanography at La Jolla, Calif., and Dr. Ebby Anyamba, a Kenyan scientist currently at the NASA Goddard Space Flight Center in Greenbelt, Md. Twenty-seven other scientists contributed to the chapter.

The new generation of computer modeling studies employs more detailed and sophisticated representations of the atmosphere than when the intergovernmental panel made its first assessment of the climate problem in 1990. Scientists' confidence in the results of the comparisons between model predictions and observations has been boosted by more powerful statistical techniques used to validate the comparison between model predictions and observations, Dr. Wigley said.

"Much of the rise in atmospheric carbon dioxide . . . is a consequence of a rise in global temperatures caused by natural factors."

Natural Factors Cause Global Warming

Frederick Seitz

The rise in the amounts of carbon dioxide and other greenhouse gases in the atmosphere is most likely due to natural causes, argues Frederick Seitz in the following viewpoint. He maintains that increases in atmospheric carbon dioxide typically follow rises in ocean temperatures. Furthermore, Seitz contends, the largest increase in average global temperature during the twentieth century occurred before the burning of fossil fuels became substantial. Seitz is the chairman of the board of directors of the George C. Marshall Institute, a consultant group on scientific and technical issues. He is also a former president of the National Academy of Sciences, the American Physical Society, and Rockefeller University in New York City.

As you read, consider the following questions:

1. What has been the total amount of global warming during the 1900s, according to Seitz?
2. How has the calculated greenhouse effect differed from actual observations of the greenhouse effect since 1880, according to the author?
3. As cited by the author, how does solar activity affect global temperatures?

Excerpted from Frederick Seitz, *Global Warming and Ozone Hole Controversies: A Challenge to Scientific Judgment* (Washington, DC: George C. Marshall Institute, 1994); ©1994 by The George C. Marshall Institute. Reprinted by permission.

Measurements show that the total amount of global warming during the last century has been about 0.5°C. Actually, such warming has been progressive since the time of the so-called Little Ice Age which occurred in the seventeenth and eighteenth centuries. Alongside this, there has possibly been an increase in greenhouse-producing gases, perhaps equivalent to a rise in the carbon dioxide content of about fifty percent. Several other gases also contribute to the greenhouse effect, including water vapor, methane, nitrous oxide, and ozone. Excluding this recent rise in greenhouse gases, the residual "natural" greenhouse effect has been sufficient in recent geological history to raise the earth's temperature by about 30°C, mainly as a result of the presence of water vapor and carbon dioxide—a highly beneficial addition as far as human health and welfare are concerned.

The major question of our time is the extent to which the warming during the past century is the result of anthropogenic [human-produced] carbon dioxide associated with the burning of fossil fuels and to what extent it is also derived from natural causes, as yet only partially understood. Moreover, there is a question as to whether such rises in greenhouse gases are in substantial part a result of the rise in temperatures, or whether the converse is true.

Carbon Dioxide Levels and Ocean Temperature

A careful statistical study of the correlation between ocean temperature and the level of carbon dioxide in the atmosphere carried out over a thirty-year period (1958–1988) by T.C. Kuo et al. of the Bell Telephone Laboratories indicates that during this period of time a rise in carbon dioxide in the air *follows* a rise in ocean temperature by about five months. In other words, it is not unreasonable on the basis of present knowledge to assume that much of the rise in atmospheric carbon dioxide over the past century is a consequence of a rise in global temperatures caused by natural factors rather than by anthropogenic additions.

Figure 1 shows the rise in temperature over the last century or so, along with a typical estimate of the rise. The estimate is derived by computer modeling. It is obtained if one associates such a rise with the combustion of fossil fuels in various forms and the greenhouse effect derived on the assumption that the gases produced by the fuels are preserved in the atmosphere.

There evidently is a large discrepancy. Among other things, most of the actual rise occurred prior to 1940 when the use of fossil fuels was relatively modest. Moreover, worldwide satellite measurements show that there has been little rise, at most of the order of 0.06°C, between 1979 and 1994, even though there has been a continuous increase in the world use of fossil fuels. . . .

Without attempting to prejudge the case, Figure 2 shows an

interesting correlation between the length of sunspot cycles and mean temperature over the same period of time as that shown in Figure 1. . . .

Carbon Dioxide Equilibrium

Any carbon dioxide which is injected into the lower atmosphere (the troposphere) comes to equilibrium with reservoirs of the gas held in molecular form in the seas and land. That CO_2 held in solution in the upper layer of the ocean is presumably the most important reservoir. Two of the questions which should be studied further concern (1) the time required for this equilibrium to come about on a global basis, and (2) the time required for the gas in the atmosphere and reservoirs to become "fixed"

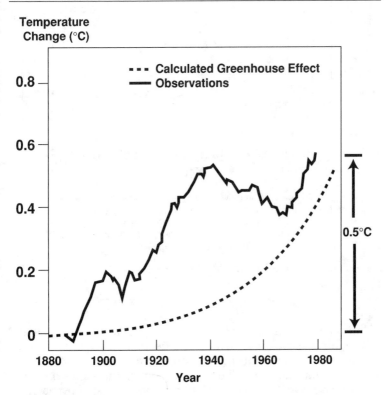

Figure 1. Calculated warming due to the increase in greenhouse gases in the last 100 years (dashed line), compared with observed temperature changes (solid line).

Frederick Seitz, *Global Warming and Ozone Hole Controversies: A Challenge to Scientific Judgment*, 1994.

in another stable chemical form in the biosphere or perhaps as a carbonate mineral on land. Current estimates on the second time, perhaps 50 years, are very rough, being closely akin to guesswork.

One answer to the first question can be obtained by studying the rate of drop in the radioactive form of carbon dioxide produced by the open-air tests of hydrogen bombs in the 1950s and early 1960s. . . .

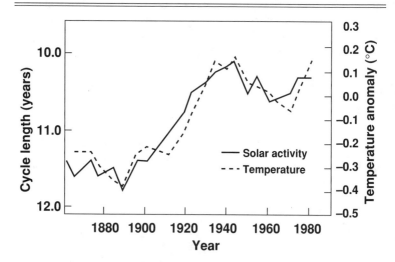

Figure 2. Comparison between global temperatures (dashed line) and solar surface magnetic activity, measured by the length of the solar cycle (solid line). The cycle length has an inverse correlation with sunspot numbers: short cycles mean high sunspot numbers and a high level of surface magnetic activity.

Frederick Seitz, *Global Warming and Ozone Hole Controversies: A Challenge to Scientific Judgment*, 1994.

The debris from the bombs was lifted into the stratosphere and requires between five and eight years to descend to the troposphere. An additional time of about five years or so is needed to achieve equilibrium. The latter time is presumably the time that would be required for carbon dioxide generated by burning fossil fuels to come to equilibrium with the intermediate global reservoir.

The results indicate that a residence time on the order of 10 years for CO_2 in the atmosphere would be more appropriate than the conventional estimate of 50 years. If this is the case, only a small fraction of the increase in atmospheric CO_2 observed in the last 100 years can be of fossil fuel origin.

In any event, the fact that we are in a relatively stable period of *global* temperature gives us time to try to understand the factors which affect that temperature with the help of appropriate experimental measurements. Hasty decisions, accompanied by radical regulatory policies, that are based on unreliable computer modeling and not on well-designed experiments, could prove very costly. Little would be lost by taking five to ten years to study the actual trends further, without adopting radical regulatory measures—a point made with clarity by M.E. Schlesinger and X. Jiang.

In brief, it appears that our planet is not in immediate danger of a runaway rise in temperature as a result of anthropogenic greenhouse gases. There is ample time to study this important issue in much more detail.

"Changes in the sun are having much more effect on the Earth's climate than carbon dioxide does."

Solar Activity Causes Global Warming

Nigel Calder

A study by two Danish scientists supports the theory that sunspots may significantly affect the Earth's climate, reports Nigel Calder in the following viewpoint. The study found that global temperature changes coincide directly with sunspot cycles, Calder writes. In addition, he notes, the study shows that solar activity coincides with global temperature changes more clearly than do carbon dioxide fluctuations. This finding, Calder says, suggests that global warming may be a natural and normal effect of variations in sunspot activity. Calder is a reporter for the liberal English newspaper the *Guardian*.

As you read, consider the following questions:

1. What is the connection between sunspots and climate change, according to Eigil Friis-Christensen and Knud Lassen, as cited by Calder?
2. How long do sunspot cycles generally last, according to the author?
3. How did the climate change when the sunspot cycle slowed between 1940 and 1960, according to Calder?

Nigel Calder, "Too Hot to Handle," *Guardian*, April 21, 1994. Reprinted by permission of Insight News & Features.

The sun is fun just now for any science watcher looking for cracks in the conventional wisdom. A billion-dollar research industry rests on a belief in global warming due to the greenhouse effect of carbon dioxide and other gases added to the air by human action. But a *samizdat* flourishes whose authors whisper that changes in the sun are having much more effect on the Earth's climate than carbon dioxide does.

If the hypothesis about the sun is correct, then the greenhouse theory, on which so many computer models and dire predictions depend, is deeply flawed. But scientifically and politically, the greenhouse bandwagon has too much momentum to bang easily to a halt.

The Sunspot Connection

In Copenhagen, Denmark, in 1991, Eigil Friis-Christensen and Knud Lassen found the connection between sunspots and climate that had eluded so many of their predecessors during the past century or so. What matters is the duration of the cycle of solar acne: The Danish scientists realized that quick cycles go with a warm climate on the Earth, and slow cycles bring chilly decades.

The count of dark magnetic blemishes on the face of the sun rises, falls, and rises again roughly every 11 years, and the last peak was in 1990. In truth, the sunspot cycle can last from nine to 13 years. During the past 100 years, the sun has shortened its cycle from 11.7 years to 9.7 years, and the global land temperature has risen by 0.6 degrees.

The analysis from Copenhagen accounted for the cooling that occurred between 1940 and 1970, which made no sense at all by the greenhouse theory of warming, because carbon-dioxide levels were rising rapidly at that time. But the solar model fit perfectly, because the sunspot cycle had slowed from 10.2 to 10.7 years between 1940 and 1960. After 1970, the sun put on a spurt and pushed up the temperature sharply enough to provoke predictions of a catastrophic warming.

No role remains for greenhouse warming when the Danish scientists extend their analysis of solar changes back in time to 1750, before the Industrial Revolution. The carbon dioxide in the air has increased by 25 percent since then, yet the Danish scientists can explain all of the changes of climate by the sun's variations, plus short-lived effects of major volcanoes. Temperature records from Northern Ireland's Armagh Observatory provide independent corroboration of their findings on climate changes in the first half of the 19th century.

The sun's magnetic behavior is still enigmatic, and the sunspot cycle is much more mysterious than it should be after centuries of study. Luckily, a new era has opened in solar research.

The sun hums to itself, and vibrations detected at the surface enable astronomers to peer into its deep interior, in much the same fashion that earthquake waves reveal the inner layers of the Earth. In 1995, the European Space Agency will station its *Soho* spacecraft on the sunward side of the Earth for an intensive campaign in solar seismology.

Sunspot Cycles and Earth Temperatures

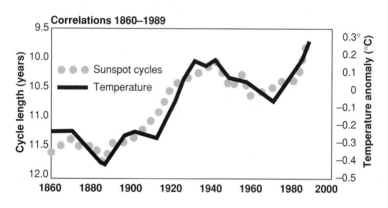

Source: Science magazine, November 1, 1991.

Further, Europe's *Ulysses* probe is already on its way to fly over the sun's southern pole and view the magnetic action from an unprecedented direction. The Japanese *Yokoh* satellite is giving X-ray images of the sun's atmosphere.

By 1996, a set of four European satellites called *Cluster* will be in orbit. They will collaborate with U.S. and Russian space missions in seeing exactly how the wind of particles from the sun interacts with the Earth's magnetism and upper atmosphere. They may help to confirm or contradict another heresy, that electrons from the sun are to blame for the thinning of the ozone layer.

"Solar variability . . . is at most a minor factor in the increase in average temperature observed over the last century."

Solar Activity Does Not Cause Global Warming

Richard A. Kerr

In the following viewpoint, Richard A. Kerr reports on a scientific study that found little evidence that variations in solar activity affect average annual temperatures. If solar activity is responsible for global warming, he writes, then the amplitude (the range between the average and extreme temperatures) of the seasonal cycle should increase. However, Kerr notes, the study showed that the amplitude is actually decreasing. According to the study, Kerr says, an increase in greenhouse gases such as carbon dioxide is the most likely cause of global warming. Kerr is a reporter for the weekly *Science* magazine.

As you read, consider the following questions:

1. What is one reason some researchers believe the sun is responsible for global warming, in Kerr's view?
2. What does a decreasing seasonal amplitude imply, according to David Thomson, as cited by Kerr?
3. What evidence does the author present to support the view that atmospheric carbon dioxide is responsible for global warming?

What is turning up Earth's thermostat? Climate researchers agree that average global temperatures have crept upward over the past century, but they are sharply divided about what is driving the rise. To most, the half-degree increase could be a first sign of a greenhouse warming, but a vocal handful have argued that the sun itself might be getting brighter. A paper in the April 17, 1995, issue of *Science*, however, could exonerate the sun—and pin the blame on greenhouse gases.

One reason that the sun has become a player in the debate over global warming is that the measured temperature rise isn't as large as some climate models predict it should be, if the increasing concentration of carbon dioxide is driving it. And at the same time, the sun has shown intriguing hints of variability that suggest that it could play a role in altering terrestrial temperatures.

Testing the Hypothesis

Although the brightness fluctuations measured in the 18 years since the first satellite-borne monitors were launched in 1977 are far too small to explain the past century's warming, indirect clues to the sun's behavior (such as the number of sunspots) suggest to some researchers that solar brightness may have fluctuated more widely in the past. But David Thomson of AT&T Bell Laboratories in Murray Hill, New Jersey, tries to sweep away some of the uncertainty. Thomson tested the climate record for a specific signature of sun-driven warming and found little trace of it. He concludes that "solar variability . . . is at most a minor factor in the increase in average temperature observed over the last century."

If Thomson is right, the rise in greenhouse gases would become the leading explanation for the warming, with some natural fluctuation within the climate system as a possible rival. "What Dave's doing is essential," says time-series analyst Jeffrey Park of Yale University, but it won't be the end of it. "If he's indeed got [the statistics] correct—and I think he does—that's going to focus people's attention on what kinds of modeling experiments should be tried" to confirm Thomson's assumptions about how the climate system works.

Thomson, a specialist in the analysis of all sorts of time series, was a stranger to the sun-climate debate until 1991, when a half-dozen colleagues sent him copies of a *Science* paper by Eigil Friis-Christensen and Knud Lassen of the Danish Meteorological Institute. That paper identified a stunningly tight correlation between the length of the sunspot cycle, which averages 11 years in length, and average temperatures in the Northern Hemisphere. The match-up implied that nearly all the warming was driven by the sun. Many climate specialists, however, were skeptical, and they hoped Thomson, with his sophisticated mathe-

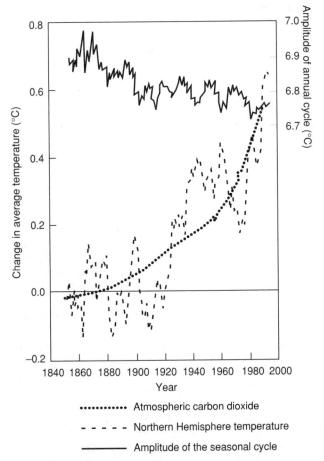

Traces of the Greenhouse?

∙∙∙∙∙∙∙∙∙∙∙∙∙ Atmospheric carbon dioxide

– – – – – Northern Hemisphere temperature

——————— Amplitude of the seasonal cycle

While atmospheric carbon dioxide and Northern Hemisphere temperature were rising together, the amplitude of the seasonal cycle declined, suggesting greenhouse gases rather than the sun as the cause.

David Thomson, *Science*, April 7, 1995.

matical tools, could put the sun-climate connection to the test.

His solution was to look at the relation between the average annual temperature over the past century and the temperature contrast between winter and summer. If a brightening of the sun were warming Earth, he reasoned, both seasons would receive additional solar heating. But because summers capture a larger share of the year's total solar input than winters do, the added solar energy and therefore the warming would be greater in summer than in winter. In that case, the amplitude [the range between the average and extreme temperatures] of the seasonal cycle should increase.

When Thomson analyzed a temperature record supplied by Philip Jones of the University of East Anglia, however, he found the opposite. While the Northern Hemisphere warmed by 0.6°C after 1900, the amplitude of the annual cycle slowly decreased rather than increased, and the pattern in the Southern Hemisphere was much the same. That flatly contradicts the behavior expected if solar brightening were at work, says Thomson. If anything, he says, the decreasing seasonal amplitude implies the sun has been dimming in this century.

Carbon Dioxide

Other features of the temperature record suggest to Thomson that, instead of the sun, increases in atmospheric carbon dioxide and other greenhouse gases are driving the warming. For one, he shows, the rise of carbon dioxide and the rise of the temperature accelerate in step during this century, as expected if one were driving the other. Thomson is also persuaded by a striking shift he found in the timing of the seasons that began around the 1940s, just when the effect of greenhouse gases would have been mounting. None of this proves an intensifying greenhouse is behind the last century's warming, says Thomson, but "you just have to take it more seriously."

Thomson says his results don't mean solar variations have played no role in climate. Another of his analyses suggests that until about 70 years ago, the sun could have shaped some shorter-term climate fluctuations. When he compared seasonal amplitude and sunspot numbers, known to increase when the sun is brighter, he found that until about 1923 they tended to increase or decrease together, suggesting that the sun's variations were helping to warm and cool Earth. But more recently, the correlation between seasonal amplitude and sunspots fell apart when greenhouse warming overwhelmed the relatively weak sun-climate connection.

72

Periodical Bibliography

The following articles have been selected to supplement the diverse views presented in this chapter. Addresses are provided for periodicals not indexed in the *Readers' Guide to Periodical Literature*, the *Alternative Press Index*, or the *Social Sciences Index*.

Joe Alper
"Putting Our Troubles to Sea," *Sea Frontiers*, Spring 1995.

Janine M. Benyus
"Bog Breath: Sleeper Factor in Global Warming," *American Forests*, March/April 1995.

Kenneth Chang
"Methane May Play Key Role in Global Warming," *Los Angeles Times*, December 14, 1995. Available from Reprints, Times Mirror Square, Los Angeles, CA 90053.

Nicholas E. Graham
"Simulation of Recent Global Temperature Trends," *Science*, February 3, 1995.

Richard A. Kerr
"Did the Tropical Pacific Drive the World's Warming?" *Science*, October 28, 1994.

Richard A. Kerr
"A Fickle Sun Could Be Altering Earth's Climate After All," *Science*, August 4, 1995.

Richard Monastersky
"Atmospheric Moisture: A Warming Sign?" *Science News*, March 11, 1995.

Richard Monastersky
"CO_2 Increase Boosts Methane Emissions," *Science News*, July 9, 1994.

Richard Monastersky
"Tropical Trouble: Two Decades of Pacific Warmth Have Fired Up the Globe," *Science News*, March 11, 1995.

Fariss Samarrai
"Little Alga Has Big Place in Global Climate," *Sea Frontiers*, Spring 1995.

Richard Stone
"Putting Methane Worries on Ice," *Science*, March 3, 1995.

David J. Thomson
"The Seasons, Global Temperature, and Precession," *Science*, April 7, 1995.

Carl Zimmer
"Unintended Consequences," *Discover*, March 1995.

What Will Be the Effects of Global Warming?

GLOBAL
WARMING

Chapter Preface

Scientists agree that Earth's average surface temperature has risen by about one degree Fahrenheit during the twentieth century. They disagree, however, about whether this warming trend will continue, and if so, how it will affect the planet and its inhabitants.

Many policymakers, scientists, and researchers believe that global warming will cause numerous catastrophic changes, including a drastic rise in sea levels. If the global average temperature continues to increase at its present rate, some scientists estimate that by 2050 sea levels will have risen between six and forty-three inches—well beyond the norm of four inches per century—due to ice melt and thermal expansion of seawater. Such a rise in sea levels would be disastrous for much of the world, these scientists maintain. Many coastal and low-lying countries would be flooded, they contend, forcing millions of people to flee their homes. In addition, they assert, barrier islands, beaches, and coastal wetlands would be destroyed, and saltwater would seep into groundwater and increase the salinity of estuaries, hurting many marine species.

Other scientists and policymakers argue that the rise in sea levels due to global warming will actually be much lower than current estimates predict. They point out that as additional scientific data has been gathered on global warming and its effects, researchers have continuously lowered the estimated amount of the sea level rise. By 2050, they claim, sea levels will probably have risen at most by six inches, which would not result in significant environmental destruction. Some researchers even maintain that global warming could cause sea levels to fall. For example, a team of American and Canadian scientists who studied the geologic history of ice caps discovered that as temperatures became warmer, the ice caps grew larger. The ice caps become larger, they explain, because warmer temperatures allow the air to hold more moisture, which results in an increase in snowfall, larger ice caps, and lower sea levels.

Whether rising temperatures will cause sea levels to change is just one of the possible effects of global warming debated by scientists and policymakers. The authors in the following chapter examine whether the effects of global warming will change Earth's climate, whether these effects will be detrimental or beneficial, and whether global warming will result in famine.

"Global warming is 'influencing the frequency and severity of natural disasters.'"

Global Warming Will Result in Major Climatic Disruptions

Der Spiegel

In the following viewpoint, the editors of the German weekly newsmagazine *Der Spiegel* assert that the average temperature of the Earth's surface and oceans is rising due to an increase in carbon dioxide emissions. This global warming is responsible for a growing number of destructive storms worldwide, they maintain, as well as other disastrous environmental changes. Unless carbon dioxide emissions are reduced, much of the Earth's climate and ecology will be adversely affected, the editors contend.

As you read, consider the following questions:

1. What evidence do the editors present to demonstrate that the Earth is being adversely affected by global warming?
2. What was the Earth like when its average temperature was three degrees warmer than it is now, according to *Der Spiegel*?
3. Why will warmer temperatures be detrimental to humans, in the editors' view?

There have been four times as many destructive storms assailing the Earth in recent years as there were in the 1960s. The number of severe low-pressure systems over the North Atlantic and Europe has doubled since 1930. Wind speeds are increasing. Property losses have gone up 10 times over—in large part because people are building increasingly expensive structures and locating them in dangerous coastal areas.

Those stuck with the bill are—not always, but usually—insurance companies. The risk involved in weather-related damage is getting harder to forecast. In the wake of Hurricane Andrew in Florida in 1992, eight insurance firms there went bankrupt. Now executives in the industry see themselves as the first victims of the greenhouse effect, which is pushing the Earth's wind machine to higher and higher speeds. "We are increasingly certain," says Gerhard Berz, a meteorologist at Münchener Rück, the world's largest reinsurance firm, that global warming is "influencing the frequency and severity of natural disasters."

According to the latest analysis in *Lloyd's List*, the British insurance newspaper, climate change is now "the main factor driving losses sky high." Some fear the very worst. If this unhealthy trend continues, warns Franklin Nutter, president of the American Reinsurance Association, "it could force the entire industry into bankruptcy."

The Evidence

Have the insurance people gone hysterical, or has climate change really seized power over the future of the Earth? Frankfurt, Germany, meteorologist Christian-Dietrich Schönwiese says that, by legal standards, those who claim that the atmosphere is warming have not yet proved their case. But there is some clear evidence:

• Glaciers are disappearing all over the world. In the Alps, the ice masses have lost half their size since the middle of the 19th century.

• Over the past 100 years, the world's sea level has risen by nearly eight inches.

• The world's oceans are getting warmer. The upper layers of water in the tropics have warmed by 0.5 degree Celsius in the past 50 years.

• El Niño, the Pacific Ocean phenomenon that causes a warm current along Peru's coast, has occurred for the last four years in a row [since 1991]. El Niño has led to crop failures in Australia and floods in California and has affected the monsoons of Southeast Asia.

Since the invention of the automobile a century ago, the layer of air around the Earth has warmed by an average of 0.7 degree Celsius. Most researchers say that much change could easily come from natural fluctuations, and it will not be possible to pinpoint human causes until the next century, if the warming continues.

But Klaus Hasselmann, head of the Max Planck Institute for Meteorology in Hamburg, Germany, and his colleagues believe that they have found a clear signal—a sharp spike in global temperature changes. Using computers, the Hamburg team has simulated the temperature fluctuations of the last 1,000 years and compared this record with the data from current warming. The result, says Hasselmann: "Current trends are unique." He wrote early in 1995 that he was "95-percent certain" that the global warming of the past 20 years has been due to human, not natural, causes.

As British and American climate experts announced in January 1995, the average global temperature in 1994 almost reached the record set in 1990—the hottest year since climate records were begun in 1850. "In this very decade," predicts American climatologist James Hansen, the average surface temperature will break all records. And all the computer simulations agree that if carbon-dioxide emissions continue to rise as they have, by the end of the 21st century at the latest, the Earth will be about three degrees warmer than it is today.

Three Degrees of Separation

At first glance, that seems merely a slight shift upward in average temperatures. But in fact it would mean a change, although gradual, unparalleled in recent millennia. The last time it was three degrees warmer than now was more than 100,000 years ago. Then, Central Europe had a climate like Africa's. And just three degrees separate today from the other climatic extreme, the last ice age of 10,000 years ago. Then, half of Europe lay under ice, and the sea level was 390 feet lower than it is today. A bitter north wind nipped at the ears of the polar bears living atop the frozen Baltic.

In human history, far smaller temperature shifts have doomed kingdoms, set off wars, forced peoples into exile, and created new religions. Since the end of the last ice age, average global temperatures have never fluctuated by more than one degree. But even such a minimal cooling may have pushed the Germanic peoples southward in A.D. 375 to destroy the Roman Empire. An average warming of just one half of one degree enabled the Vikings who settled Greenland to raise cattle and sail to America.

The next cold spell announced itself with huge storms. Floods in the Netherlands in 1212 drowned 300,000 people. This cooling, by just one degree, threw Europe and many other regions into a dark age. Summers became rainy and winters, colder. In many areas, grain would no longer ripen. Famine and epidemics raged. Humans and animals became unusually susceptible to disease, and cannibalism broke out. Average life expectancies fell by 10 years. Entire regions were depopulated.

Optimists looking at climate history draw comfort from their premature conclusion that, while cold eras have hurt humankind, warmer times have always been eras of prosperity. But the computer models leave little room for doubt that the South, especially, is in for lean years. The great heat will mean that more water will evaporate. In southern Spain and Italy, parts of Greece, large areas of Africa and the Middle East—and in the southern United States—there will be a drought like the one we see now in the African Sahel.

A Climate of Extremes

Among many scientists, there is growing concern that the world may have entered a period of dangerous climatic extremes. Although we are still in the early stages of human alteration of the atmosphere—greenhouse gas concentrations are rising at a record pace—computerized climate models suggest that these gases are likely to warm the atmosphere in the decades ahead, and may lead to a range of extreme climatic events. Droughts, floods, hurricanes, and fires, for example, could all become more common.

Christopher Flavin, *World Watch*, November/December 1994.

In the North, it will be warmer and more humid. Imagine Germany with weather like Italy's and pines and palms flourishing on islands in the Baltic. On what is now permafrost in Siberia, grain may grow, and surfing may catch on in Iceland. But climatologists do not see paradise in this picture. The additional rain that will accompany the warming will probably fall when farmers least want it. Extreme shifts in the weather will become increasingly frequent.

And people in the North will have to get accustomed to new diseases. The anopheles mosquito, the malaria vector, could once again invade Mediterranean lands such as Spain and Italy and then move north. With a three-degree global warming, say public-health experts in the Netherlands, as many as 80 million new cases of malaria could be added each year. "The spread of infectious diseases," says microbiologist Jonathan Patz of the U.S. Environmental Protection Agency, "could be the most important health consequence of global warming."

Among the losers due to climate change could be the oil, coal, and gas industries. Alternative energy sources such as wind and solar power will be better investments, analysts predict. By

2015, the climate shock will force industrial countries to introduce energy taxes or force massive cutbacks in energy use.

Catastrophic Storms

One of the effects of the greenhouse effect will hit North and South equally hard. Storms of a magnitude we have never seen will assail us. For insurance meteorologist Berz, the recent waves of increasingly frequent bad weather "are the precursors of a truly catastrophic development." It is "only a question of time" until a super-disaster comes, the storm to end all storms.

Here is what the nightmare of the insurance industry might look like: a giant cyclone with wind speeds of up to 225 miles per hour smashing downtown Tokyo or New York. Such a catastrophe could consume all of the special disaster funds of the world's reinsurance companies—about $160 billion—in one gulp. And this is a realistic possibility: When more energy is pumped into the atmosphere, the planetary wind machine speeds up. Researchers say this could add as much as 70 percent more destructive power to future storms.

Floods, like those in Europe at the end of January 1995, could become a yearly occurrence. The melting of glaciers and thermal expansion of the water in the oceans should lead to a rise in sea levels over the next century. Nearly 2 million square miles of land along coasts—an area half the size of Europe—would be put under the sea. Where will the 115 million people of Bangladesh go if large portions of their nation are transformed into mud and water?

The Calm Before the Storm

And the future could be even bleaker. Ice samples from deep within the Greenland ice bowl suggest that there may have been wild fluctuations of temperature in the Eemian Interglacial Stage, about 125,000 years ago. Once, in the course of just one decade, average temperatures fell by more than 14 degrees. This cold wave lasted 70 years and then, just as abruptly, was replaced by a very warm period that lasted many years. Then, once again, temperatures suddenly dropped.

That changes the climate outlook, for during the Eemian period, average global temperatures were three degrees warmer than today. The Eemian period was thus a historic precursor of an Earth heated by the greenhouse effect.

During the ice age that followed the Eemian Interglacial Stage, temperatures also jumped up and down. It is only over the past 10,000 years—no one knows why—that the climate has settled into a calm. Is it pure coincidence that it has been precisely during this era that humanity has conquered the globe with civilization and technology?

"There is no indication that the world is facing a climate crisis, either immediately or in the coming decades."

Global Warming May Not Result in Major Climatic Disruptions

Kent Jeffreys

Kent Jeffreys argues in the following viewpoint that the computer models that predict scenarios of climatic mayhem due to global warming are flawed. There is no evidence to support claims that global warming would spawn catastrophic storms, droughts, or other environmental disasters, he contends. Furthermore, Jeffreys maintains, a rise in global temperatures could prove to be beneficial to agriculture. Jeffreys is an environmental policy consultant and the former director of environmental studies at the Competitive Enterprise Institute, a Washington, D.C., think tank dedicated to limited government.

As you read, consider the following questions:

1. In Jeffreys's view, what are the two ways to test the accuracy of computer models?
2. What percentage of the United States is experiencing drought conditions at any time, according to the author?
3. When was the Medieval Maximum, and how did it affect the planet, in Jeffreys's opinion?

Kent Jeffreys, "Is Global Warming a Major Concern? No," *Wisconsin Counties*, March 1993. Reprinted with permission.

Since it was first suggested that the earth orbits the sun, no scientific issue has been more contentious than the debate over global warming. And no issue has raised more cries of heresy and blasphemy. Yet the environmental extremists' demands for a radical restructuring of society and the world economy threaten far greater harm than even significant warming of the climate could produce.

Unjustified Predictions

A rapid and significant increase in average temperatures, it is feared, could trigger disruptive changes in weather patterns. Some have suggested that palm trees would grow in Canada, that the ice caps would melt and inundate coastal regions, that the major crop-growing regions of the world would experience recurrent droughts or that hurricanes would become more common and more destructive. However, none of these fearsome predictions are justified.

The various global warming scenarios have been generated by computer models, which make various assumptions about the atmosphere, the oceans and their complex interaction. Developing computer models to mimic climatic interactions is incredibly difficult, and weather predictions of only a few weeks into the future are not accurate beyond broad generalities. The complexities are far greater when the predictions are for not weeks, but decades. There are two basic ways to test the accuracy of the computer models. Either wait to see if the predictions come true, or run the same program to see how well it simulates the actual climate patterns of the past century. When the latter test is applied, the computer estimates of temperatures have been significantly *above* actual measurements.

The two main thrusts of the environmental extremists' "doomsday" scenario are: 1) Rising sea levels inundating coastal regions. The millions of Third World poor living in low-lying river deltas are said to be at risk, particularly from increased storm intensity; 2) Increased drought in major crop growing regions leading to international famines.

But as the science has improved through increased knowledge, these fears have been greatly laid to rest. The rising sea level was predicted because of an assumption that large amounts of polar ice would melt. This is no longer assumed; in fact, the ice caps are apparently growing and some now argue that sea level will decline if the globe warms.

The fear of crop failure and mass starvation is similarly fading. Although approximately 25 percent of the United States is under drought conditions on any given day, this has been the case since the first Europeans arrived. These predictions of an increase in droughts are premised on the assumption that daytime temperatures would soar, greatly increasing evaporation and drying out the soil. But actual data suggests that if average temperatures have gone up at all in recent decades, it is mostly due to an increase in nighttime low temperatures. This would have the effect of lengthening the growing season by reducing the likelihood of frost and would not increase the likelihood of drought.

Overheated Fears on Global Warming

It is presumed that any change in the Earth's climate induced by human activity will be a calamitous event. This presumption is unfounded. A significant global warming is far from certain, and even the earthly changes that it would bring are hardly likely to be catastrophic.

The horrific vision of a scorched Earth and withering crops combined with monsoons of untold ferocity may help environmental lobbyists solicit donations, but this is not an accurate picture of what climate scientists expect a warmed world to be like. Most warming is likely to occur at winter and at night, creating a more benign climate, not a more hostile one.

Jonathan H. Adler, *Washington Times*, September 27, 1994.

In addition, carbon dioxide has a well-known fertilizing effect on plants including most of the major food crops. A survey of the peer-reviewed literature on plant responses to elevated levels of carbon dioxide found that 1,007 studies showed increases in plant productivity with higher carbon dioxide, 56 studies reported no change and only 24 indicated a decline in plant growth. Despite this overwhelming consensus in the scientific literature, some environmental extremists claim that some other factor, such as nutrient or moisture limitations, will alter these findings. However, the most current studies are showing even *larger* positive results when nutrients, moisture or sunlight are restricted and carbon dioxide increases. There is no reason to assume that a warmer planet with higher levels of carbon dioxide would produce less food for human consumption.

Warming Is Beneficial

In fact, to assert that today's climate is perfect is really the only alternative to admitting that warming the planet would be beneficial. The planet has only recently come out of what has been called the *Little Ice Age*. This period lasted from approximately the 1400s to 1850. (The warming trend claimed for the past century, less than one degree Fahrenheit, is well within these natural fluctuating patterns.) Yet European agriculture was particularly disrupted by these unusually cold centuries. The Little Ice Age followed a period of unusual warmth—the *Medieval Maximum*—during which the Vikings were able to colonize Greenland and even build settlements in Canada. When the colder climate returned, the settlements disappeared.

Philip H. Ableson of *Science* magazine has said of the global warming debate that "If the situation is analyzed applying the customary standards of scientific inquiry one must conclude that there has been more hype than solid facts." There is no indication that the world is facing a climate crisis, either immediately or in the coming decades. The suggestion that costly emergency responses be adopted as international policy is without merit.

It is ludicrous to suggest that the same government which cannot balance a fiscal budget can somehow balance the world greenhouse gas budget. Almost every aspect of daily life would be impacted by global warming legislation. The bureaucratic micro-management required to enforce an international carbon treaty would dwarf any in existence. The theory that such a system would actually benefit society is even weaker than the arguments supporting a global warming catastrophe.

If warming is to occur it will bring many beneficial results. Most important are the longer growing seasons and increased crop yields from carbon dioxide fertilization. The claims of worsening storms, increasing droughts and melting ice caps are frightening, but unsupported by the evidence, by calling it "uncertainty" and challenging doubters to refute each unsubstantiated claim through painstaking effort. The stakes in the global warming debate are quite high, both from the perspective of economic costs and of human liberty. Before we spend money we don't have, we should examine carefully what the environmental extremists are trying to sell.

"Unchecked [global warming] would match nuclear war in its potential for devastation."

The Effects of Global Warming Will Be Detrimental

George J. Mitchell

Carbon dioxide emissions into the Earth's atmosphere are causing a warming trend that, if left unchecked, will be detrimental to the planet's inhabitants, argues George J. Mitchell in the following viewpoint. An increase of just six degrees Fahrenheit in the Earth's average temperature would result in the flooding of coastal cities, severe drought conditions in many inland regions, and the extinction of an unprecedented number of plant and animal species, he contends. Moreover, Mitchell asserts, the economic costs of fighting the effects of global warming would be astronomical. Mitchell is a former U.S. senator from Maine and the author of *World on Fire: Saving an Endangered Earth*, from which this viewpoint is excerpted.

As you read, consider the following questions:

1. How would cities and countries be affected if the sea level rose by three feet, according to Mitchell?
2. How many families of plants may become extinct in the next one hundred years if global warming is not checked, in the author's view?
3. In Mitchell's opinion, when would the dieback of the forests begin?

From *World on Fire: Saving an Endangered Earth* by George J. Mitchell. Copyright © 1991 by Senator George J. Mitchell. Reprinted by permission of Scribner, a division of Simon & Schuster, Inc.

Sharp fluctuations in temperature are not unique on our planet. Abrupt climatic shifts have often followed shifts in the direction of earth's axis, or jumps in solar luminosity, or sudden injections of CO_2 into the atmosphere, or one-time shots of methane into the environment from geological activity, or changes in the interaction between the oceans and the atmosphere. But these don't compare with what is coming.

What will make the warming of the coming century truly unique will be the enormous velocity with which it is likely to strike. An eight-degree Fahrenheit temperature rise, for instance, would equal the entire temperature variation of the last 125,000 years: This gradual increase spread over 125 millennia would be matched within but a single century by the outpouring of greenhouse gases into the atmosphere.

What would such an unprecedented outpouring bring? What is likely to happen? The last change in world temperatures of this magnitude—the gradual warming over many millennia—transformed the landscape of North America, shifting the Atlantic Ocean inland by about a hundred miles, creating the Great Lakes, and changing the composition and location of forests throughout the U.S. Can we expect less this time?

Our Hothouse Future

The telescoping of change of such magnitude into such a short time would bring us a world far different from the one of today. It would be a world none of us would recognize. The landscape would change in ways we can't fully foresee. The earth would have an entirely new contour with an entirely new climate. And when it happens, it would be irreversible.

Here, in kaleidoscopic review, is what could happen with a six-degree Fahrenheit rise in temperature:

The earth's present climate zones and storm tracks would shift dramatically northward, driving millions of displaced people, plants, and animals with them. Thermal swelling within the seas and water from melting landborne glaciers could raise sea levels by three feet, wiping out rice fields in Asia, destroying precious coastal wetlands worldwide, drowning Venice, Cairo, Shanghai, and the Florida Keys, and threatening shorelines along every ocean side. It would cost the cities along the ocean's edge on the east coast of North America alone in the magnitude of $100 billion to hold back the threatening Atlantic. It would cost Charleston, South Carolina, protected today only by the Battery, its six-foot-high seawall and promenade, $1.5 billion to save itself from the rising sea. If nothing is done to prevent it, half of that historic city would be permanently flooded. The Netherlands, which has traditionally spent more to hold the ocean at bay behind its 250 miles of dikes and 120 miles of sand dunes than it has spent on defense, would have to take extreme measures to avoid going under—at a cost of another $10 billion. The 1,196 low-lying islands of the Maldives, only six feet above sea level at their highest point, could be swamped by a sudden storm surge with catastrophic, perhaps fatal results. The Arctic Sea could become navigable, raising profound security implications. Dramatic northward shifts in rainfall would turn the now fertile midlatitudes of the world—the breadbasket of the American Midwest—into rangeland at best, a dust bowl at worst. As much as half of the farm acreage in the southeastern United States might be lost. Monsoon patterns would shift, throwing agriculture in Asia into chaos. Ocean currents would veer to new courses, wiping out whole fisheries.

Heat Wave

Climatic extremes would trigger meteorological chaos—raging hurricanes such as we have never seen, capable of killing millions of people; uncommonly long, record-breaking heat waves; and profound drought that could drive Africa and the entire Indian subcontinent over the edge into mass starvation. By the time today's teenagers are ready to retire, the District of Columbia would be having twelve days a year of one-hundred-degree temperatures and higher; it has only one a year now. Eighty-seven days of the year would see temperatures of ninety degrees or more in the nation's capital; there are only thirty-six now. Days of 122-degree heat, such as Phoenix, Arizona experienced in the summer of 1990, could become commonplace, rather than unprecedented, in the American Southwest. Siberia and the Yukon could become the choice places on earth to live.

What such ever-rising temperatures and continued warming through a century to three centuries might bring is almost incomprehensible. A large, sustained, ever-increasing warming of earth over that long a time could melt the ice caps covering Greenland and disintegrate the West Antarctic ice sheet. The rise in sea level at that point is impossible to predict and terrible to contemplate. But it could be as high as twenty feet or more. A rise of fifteen feet would put major parts of San Francisco, New Orleans, Boston, Miami, New York, and most of the rest of the U.S. coastline under water.

The prospect for the planet under the higher temperatures and rising sea levels now predicted within our own lifetimes is sobering. . . . Even if we could stop all greenhouse gas emissions today, we would still be committed to a temperature increase worldwide of two to four degrees Fahrenheit by the middle of the twenty-first century. It would be warmer then than it has been for the past two million years. Unchecked it would match nuclear war in its potential for devastation.

The human displacement could be catastrophic, with the prospect of a thronging of tens of millions of environmental refugees over the earth as more and more areas of the planet become unfit for human habitation. A new wave of migration triggered for a whole new reason—an ongoing environmental crisis—now looms. . . .

The Rising Sea

A rising sea, caused mainly by thermal expansion of ocean waters, is a certain and far-reaching consequence of a warming world. Yet it is a consequence we have not planned for. As William D. Ruckelshaus, a former EPA [Environmental Protection Agency] administrator, has written, "We have planned our cities, developed our manufacturing techniques, and chosen our environmental protection strategies on the assumption of a stable sea level."

By the best estimate, a three-foot rise in sea level (a possibility, although a one- to two-foot rise is now more commonly predicted in a doubling of carbon dioxide in the atmosphere) would drown 25 to 80 percent of the present U.S. coastal wetlands. Unless we change our assumption of a stable sea level, from five thousand to ten thousand square miles of dry land could go under in the U.S. sometime in the next century. Without any effort to hold back the sea, most of the nineteen-thousand-mile U.S. shoreline one hundred feet from the water's edge would go under, even in the most conservative estimates. About 70 percent of the land loss would be in the Southeast, especially in Florida, Louisiana, and North Carolina. The Gulf of Mexico could surge inland into Louisiana as far as thirty miles. The eastern shore of the Chesapeake and the Delaware bays would also be hard hit. The Southeast is rich in wetlands and shore-hugging sea life. Over 85 percent of the nation's wetlands are there, 40 percent of them in Louisiana. Over 40 percent of the nation's finfish and 70 percent of its shellfish are harvested in the region.

Wetlands are not fixed in space and time. Like all living things, they can migrate—if they are not blocked, as they well might be as we scramble to protect developed shorelines from the sea. Even if not blocked, a third to two-thirds of every wetland acre in the country could be lost. If they are prevented from migrating out of harm's way by our protection of developed stretches of the coastline, the loss could be as high as eight acres out of every ten by 2030.

Twelve of the country's twenty biggest cities lie on tidal waterfronts—Baltimore, Boston, Houston, Los Angeles, Miami, New York, Philadelphia-Wilmington, San Francisco-Oakland, San Diego, Seattle, Tampa-St. Petersburg, and Washington, D.C. The cost of protecting these cities and the less populated stretches of developed shoreline from the encroaching sea would be enormous. Experts have put the price tag at $73 billion to $111 billion (in 1985 dollars) by 2100. This would pay for building bulkheads and levees, pumping sand, and raising barrier islands. It could cost as much as $50 billion to $75 billion to elevate beaches, houses, lands, and roadways on developed barrier islands. Even with these outlays an estimated seven thousand acres of dry land, an area the size of Massachusetts, could not be saved. . . .

International Flooding

Around the world cities such as Venice, Bangkok, and Taipei would be inundated. In some parts of the world subsidence would make league with the rising seas to intensify the problem. Bangladesh, a land of natural calamities, is already subsiding. A sea rising one to three feet to meet the sinking land could put 16 to 28 percent of that nation, which is little more than a mosaic of rivers on a flat and vulnerable delta, under water. Bangladesh as it is known today would virtually cease to exist. There is no higher ground for its people to move to; thirty-eight million of them could become environmental refugees.

As much as 15 percent of Egypt's teeming Nile delta could go under in a similar rising of the sea. Such a rise would inundate vast areas of the East China coastal plain, including Shanghai, China's largest port and most populated city. The Tai Hu Lake and surrounding lakes would become part of the East China Sea. Congming Island, the third largest in China, would disappear. In the face of such a rise in sea level China would have to build Netherlands-style dikes, move coastal residents inland, reorganize and rebuild its coastal industries, and relocate and replan its ocean-fronting cities and towns. . . .

Endangered Species

Extinction of species has always been with us. It is the way of life on the planet. Of all the species that have existed since the emergence of life 3.6 billion years ago, at least 90 percent have disappeared. Yet the rate of extinction of the past does not remotely compare with what we are in for in the warming world to come. The average rate of natural extinction has moved in very slow motion through the ages. It has ranged, without human intervention, from 2 to 4.6 families of species per million years, rising to an average 19.3 families per million years during the five prehistoric episodes of mass extinctions. In the next one hundred years alone we may see the unprecedented extinction of 50 families of plants—a quarter of all plant families on earth—together with many associated animal families and insects. Species in the earth's tropical forest are particularly vulnerable to what may be coming. Many delicate and specialized species in the dense, wet rain forests are incapable of surviving even a moderate disruption of their habitats. They can't even survive the depredations of human activity. They could not hope to survive a cataclysmic climate change.

The rising temperatures and the rising seas between them could wipe out entire fragile oceanic coral reef systems that are nearly as rich in their diversity of life as the rain forests. A shift in the course of the Gulf Stream, a possibility in a warming world, could, ironically, leave many species of marine life behind in waters too cold for survival. Changes in upwelling zones could sweep other marine species long accustomed to stable environments into oblivion. Moreover, all of these changes in the sea would take place in ecosystems that ecologist Norman Myers says "are beyond helping hands." James Titus, a sea-level specialist at the Environmental Protection Agency, predicts that "we'll be mere spectators in the adjustments to climate change [in the oceans]. People will have to adapt to whatever the fish decide to do."

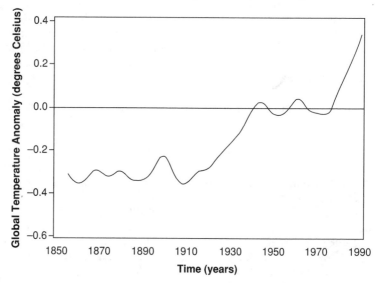

The Earth's Atmosphere Is Warming

Al Gore, *Earth in the Balance*, 1992.

For those species rooted to the earth, the toll could be particularly high and the changes over time dramatic. Over the thousands of years since the last ice age there has been a warming commensurate with what is now likely to occur in the coming century. But those temperatures rose slowly enough for the forests in the temperate zones to migrate with the change. The temperatures in the coming warming would unreasonably telescope the escape window, causing forest migrations—or diebacks—unheard of in history. It is believed that climate change on the order often predicted could move the southern boundary of the eastern hemlock, yellow birch, beech, and sugar maple range in North America four hundred miles northward. The southern pine forests could shift three hundred miles northward into the present hardwood forests of eastern Pennsylvania and New Jersey. A mass dieback of forests in the Southeast is possible. Historically, forests migrate at placid rates—on the order of six to thirty miles a century. By way of contrast, cattle egrets, which migrate on wings, can colonize an entire continent within forty years. But all too often the fastest animals can only migrate as fast as the slowest plant or animal—if those plants and animals are its main source of food.

To survive the coming earth warming many trees would have to move ten times faster than in any past migration. And in the coming flight for their lives, species will no longer have a free and clear path to safety, their way impeded only by natural barriers. Human beings, who will have triggered this mass migration, are also now blocking the way with their farmlands, highways, and cities. To a migrating forest, a city is virtually unpassable. "Few animals or plants," Robert Peters of the World Wildlife Fund has said, "would be able to cross Los Angeles on the way to the promised land."

Dying Forests

The dieback of forests would start to become noticeable after a rise in temperature of 1.5 degrees, then come with a rush. The dieback could start in thirty years and be virtually completed within sixty to eighty years. All the while these forests, unless we can help them, will be hit not only by warming, but by acid rain, and by bombardment from ultraviolet rays penetrating through the shredded ozone layer. Drier soils on the ground could trigger more frequent forest fires. Warmer temperatures could set a host of migrating pests on forests that have up to now been out of their reach. Pathogens and changes in oxidant formation could sap what resilience many of these trees have left.

As for the great rain forests of the tropical world, they could become virtually extinct by the end of this century, if the present pace of their destruction holds. We face the possibility that there could be little virgin forest left outside of the Zaire Basin, the western half of the Brazilian Amazon, the Guyana tract in northern South America, and parts of the island of New Guinea. And their days would be numbered as well, as further world demand for their products continues to quicken and the number of farms and fields and roads hewed out of the forests continues to multiply.

Computer models devised by Jagadish Shukla and Piers Sellers of the University of Maryland Center for Ocean-Land Atmosphere Interactions and Carlos Nobre of the Brazilian Space Research Institute suggest that if the rain forests become grassland within the next century—a distinct possibility—the impact on the weather worldwide could be dramatic. Rainfall in the Amazon could drop from an average one hundred inches a year to seventy-five inches. Average temperatures in the region would climb by nearly five degrees Fahrenheit. The dry season would lengthen. The chances of the forest ever returning would be slim. And world temperatures might be affected in ways we cannot now predict.

"Global warming is likely to be positive for most of mankind."

The Effects of Global Warming Will Be Beneficial

Thomas Gale Moore

Should global warming occur, it would affect the Earth in many beneficial ways, argues Thomas Gale Moore in the following viewpoint. He contends that warmer temperatures would bring milder rather than stormier weather. Furthermore, Moore maintains, global warming would create higher evening temperatures, which would lead to a longer growing season for crops. Moore is a senior fellow at the Hoover Institution and a former member of Ronald Reagan's Council of Economic Advisers.

As you read, consider the following questions:

1. How would global warming affect the manufacturing and service industries, in Moore's opinion?
2. According to the author, how would global warming affect the temperatures near the equator and the poles?
3. What conclusion does the U.S. Department of Agriculture reach about the effects of global warming on agriculture, as cited by Moore?

Excerpted from Thomas Gale Moore, "Why Global Warming Would Be Good for You," *Public Interest*, Winter 1995. Copyright 1995 by National Affairs, Inc. Reprinted by permission.

In his book *World on Fire: Saving an Endangered Earth*, Senator George Mitchell prophesied that:

> Climatic extremes would trigger meteorological chaos—raging hurricanes such as we have never seen, capable of killing millions of people; uncommonly long, record-breaking heat waves; and profound drought that could drive Africa and the entire Indian subcontinent over the edge into mass starvation. . . . Even if we could stop all greenhouse gas emissions today, we would still be committed to a temperature increase worldwide of two to four degrees Fahrenheit by the middle of the twenty-first century. It would be warmer then than it has been for the past two million years. Unchecked it would match nuclear war in its potential for devastation.

An Incorrect Forecast

Senator Mitchell's forecast and his history are both wrong. Warmer periods bring benign rather than more violent weather. Milder temperatures will induce more evaporation from oceans and thus more rainfall—where it will fall we cannot be sure, but the earth as a whole should receive greater precipitation. Meteorologists now believe that any rise in sea levels over the next century will be at most a foot or more, not twenty.

Mitchell also flunks history: around 6,000 years ago, the earth sustained temperatures that were probably more than four degrees Fahrenheit hotter than those of the twentieth century, yet mankind flourished. The Sahara desert bloomed with plants, and water-loving animals such as hippopotamuses wallowed in rivers and lakes. Dense forests carpeted Europe from the Alps to Scandinavia. The Midwest of the United States was somewhat drier than it is today, similar to contemporary western Kansas or eastern Colorado. In contrast, Canada enjoyed a warmer climate and more rainfall.

Raising the specter of disaster as well, Vice President Al Gore has called the threat of global warming "the most serious problem our civilization faces." He has styled those who dispute it as "self-interested" and compared them to spokesmen for the tobacco industry who have questioned the relation of smoking to cancer. However, Gore is misinformed; many disinterested scientists, including climatologists with no financial interest other than preventing wasteful expenditures of society's limited resources, question the evidence and the models that underlie the warming hypothesis. . . .

Expected Effects of Global Warming

Although most of the forecasts of global warming's repercussions have been dire, an examination of the likely effects suggests little basis for that view. Climate affects principally agriculture, forestry, and fishing. Manufacturing, most service industries, and nearly all extractive industries are immune to climatic shifts. Factories can be built in any climate. Banking, insurance, medical services, retailing, education, and a variety of other services can prosper as well in warm climates (with air-conditioning) as in cold (with central heating).

A few services, such as transportation and tourism, may be more susceptible to weather. A warmer climate will lower transportation costs: less snow and ice will torment truckers and automobile drivers; fewer winter storms will disrupt air travel; a lower incidence of storms and less fog will make water transport less risky. A warmer climate could, however, change the nature and location of tourism. Many ski resorts, for example, might face less reliably cold weather and shorter seasons. Warmer conditions would mean that fewer northerners would feel the need to vacation in Florida or the Caribbean. On the other hand, new tourist opportunities might develop in Alaska, northern Canada, and other locales at higher latitudes or in upper elevations.

A Blessing, Not a Curse

The benefits of global warming stagger the imagination.

The amount of arable land in the world today is principally restricted by cold and desert. Extreme global warming . . . would largely eliminate climate restrictions on land with negligible rise in sea level. Indeed, such warming would probably induce a modest drop in sea level as more water gets stored on land thereby turning deserts into "gardens.". . .

Accordingly, the author estimates that with extreme global warming . . . the world's area of arable land would triple.

Global warming—if it occurs at all—would be a blessing. It would not be the curse that our self-proclaimed environmental saviors fervently declare it to be.

Edward C. Krug, *Environment Betrayed*, January 1994.

A rise in worldwide temperatures will go virtually unnoticed by inhabitants of the industrial countries. As modern societies have developed a larger industrial base and become more service oriented, they have grown less dependent on farming, thus boosting their immunity to temperature variations. Warmer weather means, if anything, fewer power outages and less frequent interruptions of wired communications.

Only if warmer weather caused more droughts or lowered

agricultural output would even Third World countries suffer. Should the world warm, the hotter temperatures would enhance evaporation from the seas, producing more clouds and thus more precipitation worldwide. Although some areas might become drier, others would become wetter. Judging from history, Western Europe would retain plentiful rainfall, while North Africa and the Sahara might gain moisture. The Midwest United States might suffer from less precipitation and become more suitable for cattle grazing than farming. On the other hand, the Southwest would likely become wetter and better for crops.

The Effects of Warmer Temperatures

A warmer climate would produce the greatest gain in temperatures at northern latitudes, with less change near the equator. Not only would this foster a longer growing season and open up new territory for farming, but it would mitigate harsh weather. The contrast between the extreme cold near the poles and the warm atmosphere on the equator drives storms and much of the earth's climate. This difference propels air flows; if the disparity is reduced, the strength of winds driven by equatorial highs and arctic lows will be diminished.

As a result of more evaporation from the oceans, a warmer climate should intensify cloudiness. More cloud cover will moderate daytime temperatures while acting at night as an insulating blanket to retain heat. The Intergovernmental Panel on Climate Change has found exactly this pattern to hold for the last 40 years, indeed for the whole of the twentieth century. For the Northern Hemisphere in summer months, daytime high temperatures have actually fallen; but in the fall, winter, and spring, both the maximum and especially the minimum temperatures (night time) have climbed.

Warmer night-time temperatures, particularly in the spring and fall, create longer growing seasons, which should enhance agricultural productivity. Moreover, the enrichment of the atmosphere with CO_2 will fertilize plants and make for more vigorous growth. Agricultural economists studying the relationship of higher temperatures and additional CO_2 to crop yields in Canada, Australia, Japan, northern Russia, Finland, and Iceland found not only that a warmer climate would push up yields, but also that the added boost from enriched CO_2 would enhance output by 17 percent. Researchers have attributed a burgeoning of forests in Europe to the increased CO_2 and the fertilizing effect of nitrogen oxides.

A More Habitable Earth

Professor of Climatology Robert Pease writes in the *Wall Street Journal* that we may now be living in an "icehouse" world and that a warming of about two degrees Celsius, which is what his model indicates, may actually make the earth more habitable. The higher temperatures combined with more carbon dioxide will favor plant and crop growth and could well provide more food for our burgeoning global populations.

Geologic history reveals that warmer global temperatures produce more, not less, precipitation, a fact reflected by a recent scientific investigation that shows the Greenland ice cap to be thickening, not melting. So much for the catastrophic prediction that our coastlines will be flooded by a rise in sea level from polar meltwaters.

The United States Department of Agriculture, in a cautious report titled *Climate Change: Economic Implications for World Agriculture*, reviewed the likely influence of global warming on crop production and world food prices. The study, which assumed that farmers fail to make any adjustment to mitigate the effects of warmer, wetter, or drier weather—such as substituting alternative or new varieties of crops, increasing or decreasing irrigation—concludes that:

> The overall effect on the world and domestic economies would be small as reduced production in some areas would be balanced by gains in others, according to an economic model of the effects of climate change on world agricultural markets. The model . . . estimates *a slight increase* in world output and a *decline in commodity prices* under moderate climate change conditions. [Emphasis added.]

Warmer Is Better

. . . If mankind had to choose between a warmer or a cooler climate, they would be better off with the former. Whether the climate will warm is far from certain; that it will change is unquestionable. Human activity is likely to play only a small and uncertain role in these changes. The burning of fossil fuel may generate an enhanced greenhouse effect, or the release into the atmosphere of sulfates may cause cooling. It is simply hubris to believe that *Homo sapiens* can significantly affect temperatures, rainfall, and winds.

It is much easier for a rich country such as the United States to adapt to any long-term shift in weather than it is for poor countries, most of which are considerably more dependent on agriculture than the rich industrial nations. Such populations lack the resources to aid their flora and fauna in adapting, and many of their farmers earn too little to survive a shift to new conditions. These agriculturally dependent societies could suffer real hardship if the climate shifts quickly. The best preventive would be a rise in incomes which would diminish their dependence on agriculture. Higher earnings would provide them with the resources to adjust.

Preventing the predicted global warming would be very difficult, particularly since the cost of trimming emissions of CO_2 could be extremely high. William Cline of the Institute for International Economics, a proponent of regulatory initiatives to reduce the use of fossil fuels, has calculated that the cost of cutting emissions from current levels by one-third by 2040 would be 3.5 percent of World Gross Product. In terms of the estimated level of world output in 1992, this would amount to roughly $900 billion annually, an amount that could slow growth and impoverish some who survive on the margin. These resources could be better spent on promoting investment in the poorer countries of the world.

Should warming become apparent at some time in the future, creating more difficulties than benefits, policy-makers may have to consider preventive measures. Global warming is likely to be positive for most of mankind while the additional carbon, rain, and warmth should also promote plant growth that can sustain an expanding world population. Global change is inevitable—warmer is better, richer is healthier.

"People in already impoverished tropical and subtropical countries are likely to face more starvation and malnutrition than ever before."

Global Warming May Cause Famine

David E. Pitt

Researchers studying global warming expect the rising temperatures to affect agriculture worldwide. In the following viewpoint, David E. Pitt reports on a scientific study by Cynthia Rosenzweig and Martin L. Parry that predicts massive crop failures in developing countries due to global warming. According to Pitt, the study reveals that although some agricultural areas may benefit from warmer and longer growing seasons, many others—primarily those in developing countries—may experience severe famines. Pitt is a former reporter for the *New York Times*.

As you read, consider the following questions:

1. How much are average temperatures expected to rise, according to Pitt?
2. According to the author, how is the Rosenzweig-Parry study different from other global warming studies?
3. In what ways would the effects of global warming damage crops in developing countries, according to the study, as cited by the author?

Using a combination of computer models, an international team of scientists investigating the effects of global warming on agriculture has summoned up a detailed vision of the future that will cheer farmers and commodity traders in the northern latitudes, but not people in developing countries.

Experts say the three-year study is apparently the first in what is likely to be a torrent of interdisciplinary, computer-assisted projections of the myriad biophysical and socioeconomic consequences of climate change.

The study predicts that rising temperatures resulting from greenhouse gas emissions will cause only a "slight to moderate" decline in world grain production, causing prices to rise, but leaving most industrial nations more or less unharmed—and actually increasing crop production in some.

But people in already impoverished tropical and subtropical countries are likely to face more starvation and malnutrition than ever before, despite the best efforts of farmers to counter the effects of rising temperatures on their harvests, according to the study's principal authors, Dr. Cynthia Rosenzweig of Columbia University and the Goddard Institute for Space Studies, and Prof. Martin L. Parry, director of the Environmental Change Unit at Oxford University in England.

Efforts to Assess Risks

The study was published a month before the more than 150 governments that have signed the 1992 United Nations treaty to combat global warming [were] to gather for talks in Geneva in February 1994.

Until recently, much of the advanced research on climate change focused on whether significant global warming was likely to occur at all. This debate is far from settled, but many scientists are convinced that without drastic measures to reduce the burning of fossil fuels, average temperatures are likely to rise 3 to 8 degrees Fahrenheit by the year 2100. Efforts are turning more and more to making precise assessments of the likely risks if this turns out to be the case.

Earlier computer models of climate change predicted similarly disparate effects on crop yields, with some northerly regions benefiting while developing countries suffered. But until the Rosenzweig-Parry study, other scientists say, no assessment had incorporated so many variables into a series of precise, comprehensive predictions.

"They've done a terrific job in gradually learning about the agricultural system and how it might change, then building models that will simulate those changes," said Dr. Michael Oppenheimer, a senior scientist at the Environmental Defense Fund, an advocacy group. "Any one scenario that they ran might not tell you much, but they've run a lot of them, and the sort of underlying themes which emerge within the broad range of uncertainty tell you something about what the future may actually look like."

The Environmental Protection Agency, which largely financed the project with technical help from the United States Agency for International Development, is also sponsoring studies on the effects of global warming on natural ecosystems, human health, river basins and the rise of sea levels.

More Hunger in Developing Nations

Estimated additional number of people (in millions) at risk of hunger in 2060

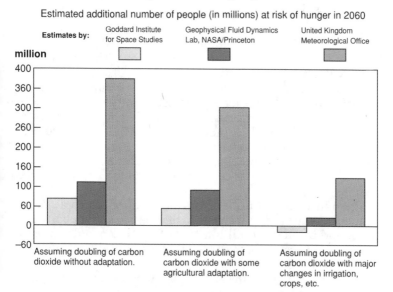

Cynthia Rosenzweig and Martin L. Parry, *Nature*, January 13, 1994.

The Rosenzweig-Parry findings, published in the January 13, 1994, issue of the British journal *Nature*, involved 60 economists, agronomists and atmospheric scientists from 25 countries who helped prepare "general circulation" models of the atmosphere; global food-trade patterns and crop growth in 18 countries, 12 of them in the developing world.

The study used crop-yield data supplied by agronomists from Argentina, Australia, Bangladesh, Brazil, Canada, China, Egypt, France, India, Japan, Mexico, Pakistan, the Philippines, Thailand, Russia, the United States, Uruguay and Zimbabwe. The crop figures were then examined under three different models of climate change. The researchers then juxtaposed the data with world food-trade projections to obtain a picture of how many people would be put at risk of hunger.

Developing Countries Will Be Hit the Hardest

The study found that although the amount of warming was expected to be highest in the northern latitudes, harming some growing areas and expanding others, the effect on crops was likely to be more uniformly severe in the southern latitudes. This is because the basic subsistence crops the study looked at, including wheat, maize, rice and soybeans, would not fare as well under the stress caused by increased heat and higher evaporation rates.

"This is the most surprising part of our study," Dr. Rosenzweig said. "It shows that even with lower amounts of warming, the vulnerability of the low-latitude places, where developing countries tend to be located, is very much present. The high temperatures will push the crops very near the edge."

According to the study, crop yields will be stunted by higher temperatures and damaged by increased difficulty in retaining water. And, because increased heat accelerates the growth cycle, the crops that will be produced will have less time to accumulate carbohydrates and are thus less nutritious.

The study says the problem will be compounded by sharp increases in world cereal prices resulting from the climate-induced declines in harvests.

"These increases in price affect the number of people at risk of hunger," the study said, noting that because of global warming, an additional 60 million to 350 million people, most of them in the developing world, could face critical food shortages by the year 2060.

The study also found that although the presence of heightened levels of carbon dioxide in the atmosphere would increase crop productivity in the northern latitudes by enhancing photosynthesis rates, its beneficial effects would probably be limited in the southern latitudes by the damaging effects of heat. . . .

Dr. Rosenzweig acknowledged that "further research clearly needs to be done on other crops that are very important in these [tropical] areas, things like cassava and millet."

"The real strength of our study was that it was interdisciplinary," Dr. Rosenzweig said. "There's a move to make very integrated models now, and have one model do everything. I like our approach, in which we let the state-of-the-art models in each discipline handle each of the three aspects, and then we work together as scientists to see where the linkages are."

"*The future can be one without famine or malnutrition, regardless of whether and how the climate changes.*"

Global Warming May Not Cause Famine

John Reilly

In January 1994, researchers Cynthia Rosenzweig and Martin L. Parry published a study in which they argued that global warming may cause famine in developing countries. In the following viewpoint, John Reilly argues that Rosenzweig and Parry's study was overly pessimistic. He contends that their research did not take into account many variables that could prevent a country from suffering famine due to global warming. If countries make an effort now to eliminate poverty and famine, Reilly maintains, it is unlikely that global warming will cause famines in these countries in the future. Reilly is a member of the Economic Research Service in Washington, D.C.

As you read, consider the following questions:

1. What are the three main faults that make Rosenzweig and Parry's study overly pessimistic, according to Reilly?
2. Why does famine occur, in the author's opinion?
3. What solutions would eliminate famine and malnutrition, in Reilly's view?

John Reilly, "Crops and Climate Change." Reprinted by permission from *Nature*, vol. 367, January 13, 1994, p. 118. Copyright ©1994 Macmillan Magazines Ltd.

Will global climate change over the next century seriously limit agricultural production and cause widespread famine? Cynthia Rosenzweig and Martin L. Parry investigate this possibility and find that although the location of food production may shift, global food prospects do not worsen significantly. There seems to be no 'disaster threshold' for global food production.

This finding is at odds with the language of the Framework Convention on Climate Change, which calls for the world to curb emissions and avoid dangerous greenhouse gas concentrations. The notion of a threshold implies that there is some level of trace gases where the effects are so devastating that we must avoid it at whatever cost, but that we can edge up to this limit as long as we do not exceed it. With the emphasis instead on adjustment and relocation of agricultural production, the debate on climate-change policy shifts to manageable rates of change and to concerns about the responsibility of the world community towards those areas that suffer significant losses.

Impacts

Rosenzweig and Parry's work looks at the agricultural effects to be expected from temperature and precipitation changes associated with a doubling of atmospheric carbon dioxide concentration (or equivalent trace gases), together with the effects of direct 'CO_2 fertilization'. They investigate three different general circulation models (GCMs), each of which gives a change of several degrees in mean global temperature in the next century, and go on to look at crop yields, possible adaptations and a model of world food trade.

Theirs is the first extensive effort to produce a consistent estimate of the impacts of climate change worldwide from specific GCM scenarios. Earlier work tested sensitivities and relied on disparate estimates of the impact on crop yields with, for many areas of the world, very limited information. The basis of this study is similar, however, in that it relies on detailed crop growth models for specific geographical points. These few points form the basis for extrapolating to states or provinces, nations and regions. The suite of crop response models used by Rosenzweig and Parry was limited to a few (important) grain crops, the results being extended to other crops with reference to the literature. An alternative approach would be to use databases of global geographical information, such as global climate and soils, to estimate crop potential on the basis of the specific climate in each grid and estimates of how that climate will change.

Adaptation was introduced according to the judgement of local agricultural scientists in each participating country. As such, adaptation response was only as creative and complete as the imagination of the agronomist concerned. Any small group of individuals studying the situation today is unlikely to foresee the full range of possible adaptations—crop breeding, technical advances and more—that might be developed over a hundred years of gradually changing climate. Further, agronomists in the team generally experimented with adaptations at only the most affected site in their country (or region of responsibility). As a simplification, yield losses were halved for the nation if adaptation was partial, and set to zero if it was complete, so that adaptation never outweighed losses. But if adaptation measures could completely or nearly completely offset losses at the most severely affected sites, the same adaptation might well lead to yield increases at the less severely affected sites.

The Impact on Crops

It is widely believed that global warming would lead to droughts while increasing the water requirements of plants. But this theory does not stand up to scrutiny. First, droughts are not likely to increase with global warming if the primary effect is to raise only night-time temperatures. Second, since water evaporation from plants mainly occurs during the day, plants would not experience greater heat stress simply from warmer nights.

John Shanahan, *Heritage Foundation Backgrounder*, May 21, 1992.

Rosenzweig and Parry's view that farmers will only try to maintain yields against losses but not adapt to increase them is probably over-pessimistic. The Green Revolution and the long-term trend of productivity growth (roughly 2.1 per cent per annum) in US agriculture both testify that farmers will try to increase yields if it pays them to do so. A fuller consideration of adaptation may show that, globally, several of the GCM scenarios could give overall increases in production.

Moreover, the focus on crops that are staples of temperate agriculture may have led to an overestimate of the negative impacts in tropical regions. Thus, their conclusion that developing countries will be more severely affected, although compelling, remains open to further investigation using methods that can consider beans, root crops, sugar cane, and various fruit and vegetable crops better suited to warm climates.

Finally, the economic impact of agricultural changes may strongly depend on whether a country is an agricultural exporter or importer. Agricultural exporting countries fared well during the 1970s when various world commodity prices were high. If climate change leads to high agricultural prices, then developing countries such as Thailand or Argentina, which are major agricultural producers and exporters, could do well, whereas major consuming areas, regardless of the direct impact of climate on agriculture in the region, could suffer. Tempting as it is to simplify the world into 'developed' and 'developing' nations, this may give a misleading picture of the impact on individual countries.

Hunger

A unique contribution of Rosenzweig and Parry's study is the attempt to link the risk of hunger specifically with climate projections. It is generally recognized that current food production capacity is adequate to avoid famine and malnutrition, but famine occurs because available food does not always get to those most in need. Wars and political upheaval are the primary cause of current famines (as in Somalia and Bosnia). In other words, famine and food shortage is a short-term, unexpected (although recurring) phenomenon, whereas climate change is a long-term trend, at least as described by the current generation of GCMs. This trend may, indeed almost certainly will, exacerbate famine potential in some areas. As Rosenzweig and Parry demonstrate, many local production changes may create a global picture of sufficient food, but regional populations continue to be very vulnerable to famine.

This agricultural study contains the core of a debate that will play out in the current Intergovernmental Panel on Climate Change and future negotiations on the Framework Convention. Certainly, it seems callous to balance the human catastrophe of famine, with thousands of deaths and severe malnutrition, against an economic cost of dollars per tonne of carbon. Shouldn't the humanitarian spirit be willing to spend the necessary money to limit emissions and avoid these potential famines? But from our current experience we know that current famines are a choice, not an inevitability built of too little food.

Cost-Benefit Calculations

Given the possibility (but not assurance) of redistributions of resources to mitigate the locally severe effects of climate change, rational cost-benefit calculations cut little ice in the international negotiations on climate change. Those who see their prospects for famine or coastal destruction increasing will find little comfort in the assurance that the increase in trace gases is consistent with a balancing of costs and benefits. At the same time, the world as a whole can ill afford an extremely costly effort to control emissions if the effects are locally severe but reasonably cheap, in principle, to compensate. Such funds might save far more lives if they were spent on AIDS research, eliminating water-borne diseases or improving childhood nutrition.

For a reasoned climate change policy to be agreed, those at particular risk must have some assurance that their unavoided losses will be compensated. This is not a straightforward exercise. It will be difficult to separate the drought or hurricane attributable to climate change from the drought or hurricane that would have occurred anyway. It seems that for the world to deal with the problem of climate change rationally, it must be prepared to provide a basic level of security to all its citizens.

The long horizon of climate change, with the potential for famine to increase, suggests that now is the time (if one needed another reason) to make a concerted effort to eliminate famine and malnutrition. Poverty, subsistence agriculture, poorly developed social support networks and weak governmental processes appear to be their preconditions; training, improved health delivery, education, economic development and improved agriculture production techniques are their solution. With success the future can be one without famine or malnutrition, regardless of whether and how the climate changes.

Periodical Bibliography

The following articles have been selected to supplement the diverse views presented in this chapter. Addresses are provided for periodicals not indexed in the *Readers' Guide to Periodical Literature*, the *Alternative Press Index*, or the *Social Sciences Index*.

T. Adler	"As the Globe Warms, Keep an Eye on Storms," *Science News*, January 7, 1995.
Wilfred Beckerman and Jesse Malkin	"How Much Does Global Warming Matter?" *Public Interest*, Winter 1994.
Sharon Begley	"He's Not Full of Hot Air," *Newsweek*, January 22, 1996.
Gregg Easterbrook	"The Good Earth Looks Better," *New York Times*, April 21, 1995.
Mike Hulme and Mick Kelly	"Exploring the Links Between Desertification and Climate Change," *Environment*, July/August 1993.
Richard A. Kerr	"Studies Say—Tentatively—That Greenhouse Warming Is Here," *Science*, June 16, 1995.
Jeremy Leggett	"Global Warming: The Worst Case," *Bulletin of the Atomic Scientists*, June 1992. Available from 6042 S. Kimbark Ave., Chicago, IL 60637.
Mark Nichols	"Feeling the Heat," *Maclean's*, April 24, 1995.
A. Barrie Pittock	"Climate Change and World Food Supply," *Environment*, November 1995.
S. Fred Singer	"Benefits of Global Warming," *Society*, March/April 1992.
S. Fred Singer	"Warming Theories Need Warning Label," *Bulletin of the Atomic Scientists*, June 1992.
Gary Taubes	"Is a Warmer Climate Wilting the Forests of the North?" *Science*, March 17, 1995.
World Press Review	Special section on global warming, July 1995.
Carl Zimmer	"Good News and Bad News," *Discover*, May 1994.

Should Measures Be Taken to Combat Global Warming?

GLOBAL
WARMING

Chapter Preface

At the United Nations Conference on Environment and Development (the Earth Summit) held in Rio de Janeiro in June 1992, participating countries agreed to help combat global warming by reducing their greenhouse gas emissions to 1990 levels by the year 2000. In 1995, more than one hundred of the Earth Summit signatories met in Berlin to negotiate a new set of goals for reducing carbon emissions. The Berlin Mandate includes a measure called joint implementation, a plan that would allow industrialized countries to accumulate credits toward meeting their own emission-reduction quotas by helping developing countries lower their carbon emissions.

Supporters of joint implementation believe that the plan will encourage firms to implement measures that will reduce the most greenhouse gas emissions at the lowest cost. Canadian economist Erik Haites maintains that joint implementation measures will allow countries to "get the lowest overall cost of reaching whatever goal, be it stabilization or a given reduction in emissions." Furthermore, he contends, when a business in an industrialized country implements measures to reduce the greenhouse gas emissions in a developing country, the developing country will benefit from both the carbon emissions reduction and the transfer of the technology used to lower the emissions.

Many environmental groups oppose the joint implementation plan, however. Developed countries produce more greenhouse gas emissions than developing countries, they argue. Therefore, they assert, the industrialized countries should be required to reduce their own greenhouse gas emissions rather than receiving credits for the easier task of decreasing the already low emissions of small developing countries. Many delegates of developing countries also oppose the joint implementation plan. They fear that if their countries are later asked to further reduce their emissions, only expensive options will be left because industrialized nations will have already used the low-cost reduction measures in order to gain credits under the joint implementation plan. "According to researchers Reinhard Loske and Sebastian Oberthur, "joint implementation is no panacea for the protection of the climate."

Joint implementation is just one plan the members of the United Nations Conference on Environment and Development and other researchers have proposed to try to control global warming. The authors in the following chapter debate this and other efforts to reduce greenhouse gas emissions and what effect these measures would have on the world's economy and environment.

"In order to stop the accumulation of greenhouse gases . . . carbon emissions will have to be reduced to . . . 60 to 80 percent below today's rate."

Carbon Emissions Should Be Reduced

Christopher Flavin and Odil Tunali

Gases in the Earth's atmosphere—particularly carbon dioxide—trap solar heat and keep the planet warm enough for habitation. In the following viewpoint, Christopher Flavin and Odil Tunali argue that industries around the world are emitting excessive amounts of carbon dioxide, which may result in a dangerous and unprecedented rise in atmospheric temperatures. They maintain that reducing carbon emissions to 1990 levels—a step advocated by a global climate treaty—is not enough to prevent catastrophic global warming. Countries must drastically cut their carbon emissions now or the world will face disastrous climatic changes in the future, the authors contend. Flavin is the vice president for research at the Worldwatch Institute, an environmental research organization. Tunali is a staff researcher with Worldwatch.

As you read, consider the following questions:

1. Which countries have the highest carbon emissions, according to the authors?
2. In Flavin and Tunali's opinion, which groups most strongly oppose efforts to combat global warming?
3. According to the authors, what is the equivalent of a carbon dioxide concentration of 359 parts per million?

In June 1992, when the leaders of 106 nations met at the Earth Summit in Rio de Janeiro to sign the Framework Convention on Climate Change, it seemed that governments were finally taking action on what may be the ultimate global threat. Diplomats had been preparing the climate treaty for four years, and a host of studies had confirmed the dangers of global warming, as well as the need to begin cost-effectively reducing emissions of carbon dioxide and other greenhouse gases.

The Berlin Meeting

After nearly three years of additional preparation, more than 100 nations have ratified the Rio treaty, and in late March 1995, their diplomats—along with thousands of reporters and lobbyists—will convene in Berlin for the first "Conference of the Parties." The purpose of the Berlin meeting is to proceed with the myriad details of implementing the climate treaty, and to consider proposals for strengthening it. Sadly, the officials who gather in Berlin will have to face the reality that so far, the treaty has had little effect, and the world is still far from turning the climate problem around.

Although industrial countries were expected to be well along in slowing their emissions of greenhouse gases by now, most have interpreted the treaty's ambiguous targets in ways that require no disruptions of their favored industries; many still give enormous subsidies to oil and coal, and none have adopted sizable carbon dioxide taxes. . . .

Meanwhile, far from abating, global emissions have continued to rise, even in the industrial countries where emissions are highest; and in the burgeoning economies of Asia and Latin America they are on pace to double by 2009. Nearly 9 billion more tons of carbon have accumulated in the atmosphere just since Rio, and evidence of climate change mounts. Some scientists are even worried about a possible connection with the catastrophic series of storms and floods that has caused record financial losses in many parts of the world in the early 1990s. . . .

Efforts to stabilize the climate have run into a stiff headwind of opposition from some of the world's most powerful industries and labor groups: those that extract, process, and sell fossil fuels. From the American Petroleum Institute to the Saudi Arabian government and the German coal mining union, a powerful array of interests has organized to fight climate policies at the national and international levels. . . .

Rio and Beyond

The Framework Convention on Climate Change has perhaps the most ambitious long-term goal of any environmental treaty—not only reducing the total annual emissions of greenhouse gases worldwide, but stabilizing the overall concentration in the atmosphere. The importance of this goal has been acknowledged by almost every government, at least in principle; by the end of 1994, the convention had been signed by 166 nations and ratified by 116.

But the convention is only a framework, and imposes minimal obligations on its signatories. Parties are obliged only to develop inventories of greenhouse gas emissions, prepare "national programs" for mitigating and adapting to climate change, and "take climate into consideration" when formulating other governmental policies.

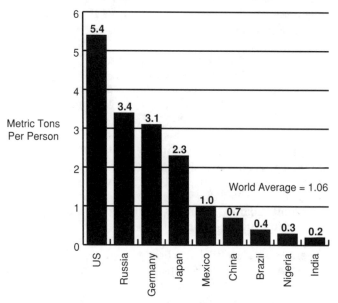

Carbon Emissions Per Capita from Fossil Fuel Burning, Selected Countries, 1993

Christopher Flavin and Odil Tunali, *World Watch*, March/April 1995.

Before Rio, the biggest debate was over whether industrial countries should be *required* to curb their emissions of greenhouse gases. Most nations favored such a mandate, but the vehement opposition of the United States resulted in a weak, last-minute compromise: the convention calls on industrial countries to take the lead in limiting emissions, and suggests—but does not require—that they return emissions to the 1990 level or below in the year 2000. . . .

The gradual shift from "binding limits" to vague "national targets" and "goals" has turned this portion of the treaty into a sham. And in any case, countries representing only about half of global greenhouse gas emissions have committed to goals of any kind. As allowed under the treaty, most nations in Asia, Latin America, and Africa have not adopted any significant climate goals or programs—and in most cases their greenhouse gas emissions are soaring.

Yet despite this feeble record, much of the discussion leading up to Berlin has revolved around whether to tighten these "targets" or extend them beyond 2000. Many environmental groups, together with 35 small island states that say rising seas could wipe them out, have recommended strong new protocols to the treaty. They would require that industrial countries reduce their emissions in the year 2005 to at least 20 percent below 1990 levels. Germany also supports a post-2000 protocol, but backed away from endorsing any specific figures in 1994, when some industries objected.

While such strengthening of the Rio climate treaty is essential to meet its long-run goal of stabilizing the atmosphere, a more immediate question must first be addressed: how to ensure that all targets are treated with respect—and lead to real changes in industrial and consumer behavior.

The Carbon Keeps Building

A review of recent energy trends shows some alarming developments. The sharp decline of the energy-intensive economies of Eastern Europe and the former Soviet Union helped restrain global carbon dioxide emissions in the early nineties, but that only served to obscure the rapid growth of emissions occurring elsewhere.

Between 1990 and 1994, carbon emissions from fossil fuels rose 3 percent in Western Europe and 5 percent in North America, together representing a roughly 100 million ton increase in the global total—equivalent to the annual output of Brazil. The developing world, meanwhile, is in the midst of a carbon boom. Between 1990 and 1993, emissions rose 8 percent in Brazil, 13 percent in India, and 16 percent in Turkey. China has increased its emissions by more than 80 percent since 1980, and by 1994, it had become the world's second largest emitter.

After discounting the temporary declines in Eastern Europe, it appears that the underlying rate of growth in global carbon emissions is now 2 to 3 percent per year. Although this represents a slowdown from the pre-oil crisis days of the 1960s, it is still a trend that is moving dangerously in the wrong direction.

Fossil fuel burning is now releasing about 6 billion tons of carbon into the air each year, along with additional amounts from the continuing loss of forest cover in many nations. As a result, some 3 billion tons of carbon accumulate in the atmosphere each year—the rest being absorbed by oceans and forests. The problem is further exacerbated by the release of several more minor gases that also add to the greenhouse effect.

By 1995, carbon dioxide concentrations in the atmosphere have reached about 359 parts per million, representing a 170 billion ton increase in this warm blanket of gases that has accumulated since the beginning of the industrial revolution. This is equivalent to placing a 2-megawatt engine (the size of a bus engine) on every square kilometer of the earth's land and water surface. Altogether, these greenhouse gases trap as much heat as would be generated by more than 300,000 large nuclear power plants. And as more carbon dioxide is released, the heat continues to build.

In order to stop the accumulation of greenhouse gases and allow the earth to return to equilibrium over a period of centuries, scientists say that carbon emissions will have to be reduced to the rate at which the oceans can absorb it, or 60 to 80 percent below today's rate. Yet, on the current path, emissions are projected to *increase* by 60 percent within the next two decades. If developing countries were later to reach even half of current industrial country per capita emissions levels, global emissions would triple.

Substantial Risks

Although the exact amount of warming and the resulting regional effects cannot be predicted precisely, the risks are substantial. Scientists believe that a warmer climate could produce more severe droughts, stronger hurricanes, and more destructive floods. Such changes could undermine food production and cause catastrophic fires that would destroy large forests. Rising seas could flood many coastal cities and islands, and put millions of lives at risk. The costs of such changes could reach hundreds of billions of dollars, according to a study by the International Institute for Economics.

In other words, even a stringent interpretation of the treaty's goals—freezing industrial country emissions at the 1990 level after the year 2000, and then enforcing the freeze—is far from adequate. Stabilizing the earth's atmosphere will require sharp *cuts* in industrial country emissions, and a rapid slowdown in emissions growth in developing nations. With such targets in mind, none of the nations gathering in Berlin can be sanguine about the progress they have made so far.

*"Forcing abatement [of carbon emissions] now
. . . would be expensive, inefficient and almost
certainly wrong."*

Carbon Emissions Should Not Be Reduced

William F. O'Keefe

William F. O'Keefe is the executive vice president of the American Petroleum Institute, a research and advocacy organization for the petroleum industry. In the following viewpoint, O'Keefe argues that not enough is known about global warming to justify the economic burdens that would be caused by reducing carbon dioxide emissions. There is no scientific consensus on the need for immediate reductions of carbon emissions, he maintains. In fact, O'Keefe contends, many scientists assert that actions to combat global warming can be safely delayed until more is known about the phenomenon.

As you read, consider the following questions:

1. According to the author, what are some of the mistakes being made in global warming research?
2. What would be some of the economic implications of delaying the reduction of carbon emissions, in O'Keefe's opinion?
3. What five proposals does the author advocate for addressing the problem of global warming?

Excerpted from William F. O'Keefe, "Time for a Reality Check," keynote address, International Conference on Climate Change, Washington, D.C., May 22, 1995. Reprinted by permission.

is nothing so powerful as a plausible but false idea. Global warming may turn out to be a reality but right now there also are enough reasons to conclude that what is masquerading as the most serious of environmental threats may be just another hobgoblin being used to advance agendas that can't survive on their own merits.

Challenging the Process

I want to be absolutely clear that I am *not* asserting that the global warming threat is a hoax. I am challenging the process —the way it is being addressed. Instead of rational debate, what we have is advocacy driven by pseudo-science and hyped by the media. The current approach will eventually be seen as flawed because politicizing such an important environmental issue— and that's clearly what's been done—subverts rational policy-making and threatens to impose unreasonable burdens on the public. Ted Koppel made that point with Vice President Al Gore [in 1993] on this very issue, and I quote, "The measure of good science is neither the politics of the scientist nor the people with whom the scientist associates. It is the immersion of hypothesis into the acid of truth. That's the hard way to do it, but it's the only way that works."

Right now, no one knows enough about global warming to advocate with certainty the kinds of actions that could jeopardize our economic well-being, and the economic aspirations of developing countries. That doesn't mean no action, which is usually described pejoratively and erroneously as "business as usual." It does mean actions must be based on facts, not misperceptions and myths. It does mean a mindset that reexamines, rethinks and changes course based on new knowledge. This is what former arms control negotiator Paul Nitze called, "working the problem," subjecting it to exhaustive examination, discussing it from many angles and being willing to go over it repeatedly until it yields a solution.

In short, I am advocating a reality check on the process based on the . . . scientific and economic realities. Each of these realities has an important role in determining how we respond to the global warming threat. Our goal should be to identify actions that do the least damage to material well-being and that preserve the path to a better way of life, especially for the developing nations.

What we have instead is a process driven by political gamesmanship that will devolve into beggar-thy-neighbor policies reminiscent of eighteenth-century mercantilism. What has taken place between [the 1992 Earth Summit in] Rio de Janeiro and [a follow-up conference in 1995 in] Berlin has been so "wooden-headed" that a Martian observer would report back that intelligent life does not exist on earth. . . .

Those who advocate deep emission reductions contend that a scientific consensus exists and that man-made emissions of greenhouse gases will lead to a dangerous level of global warming. That's simply wrong. For example, it's been demonstrated that uncertainty about variations in water vapor can overwhelm models that are used for policy recommendations. According to the various polls that have been taken of climate experts, no more than 40 percent support the premise that man-induced warming is now underway. That is hardly a consensus. . . .

I just want to point out that those who raise questions are not saying that the threat is not real or serious. They are questioning the analytical and scientific foundation for political statements and the exaggerated estimates of future climate change. . . .

A Counter-Productive Effect

Measures to curb CO_2 pollution may still be justified in terms of energy conservation. But there is little scientific basis for believing that they will prevent undesirable climate change even if they do restrict future greenhouse warming.

For example, cutting back on power-plant emissions to control acid rain and CO_2 pollution may have an unintended counter-productive effect. Sulfate aerosols don't last long in the atmosphere. Cut back their production and their cooling influence would quickly diminish. If they have been masking greenhouse warming in some areas, "there's a possibility of getting a warming spurt," says climate analyst Jeffrey Kiehl.

Robert C. Cowen, *Christian Science Monitor*, September 14, 1994.

Based on the theory that action equates to progress, leadership, valuable time, energy and money are being wasted on frequent international meetings to review the state of climate science and meet perceived policy needs. This is ridiculous. Any serious student of science knows that the production of new knowledge is time consuming and can't be scheduled like next year's vacation. We would be much better off if these resources were used to improve the understanding of climate, address major data gaps and generate new knowledge over a realistic time frame. Instead, as the mystical year 2000 draws closer, we are more likely to have expertise in fine wines and exotic meeting locales than in the impact of mankind's activities on the global climate.

Solid and defensible scientific research takes time. It takes funding. And it needs to be guided by the policymakers' need for answers—independent of the political process. As David Sugden of Edinburgh University recently observed, "Science should not be a campaigning enterprise but should be measuring the evidence, seeking the truth."

In the United States, we've made mistakes we should learn from. We spent ten years and half-a-billion dollars on the National Acid Precipitation Assessment Program (NAPAP)—which produced meaningful scientific advances, but ultimately failed in its primary mission—to provide timely, policy-relevant information to guide the development of the Clean Air Act. Instead, costly policies were enacted into law that do not address real problems.

And yet, global warming research is headed down the same path. There has been no serious effort to define the research priorities, to insist on integrated assessments, to ensure independent science and to require peer-review—not peer-review by press release. We need a process to shape appropriate projects and set realistic timetables, so that questions are answered in a meaningful, and timely, way. I was pleased, therefore, to hear [State Department Undersecretary for Global Affairs Timothy] Wirth's announcement about the Clinton Administration's plans for a more integrated approach to assessment.

Delay Will Have Little Effect

To expect the citizens of this nation, or any nation, to implement actions that disrupt their economies without solid answers to the most pressing questions ignores the limits of what is at best a forced consensus among a well-organized and vocal minority. Especially when there will not be a serious penalty for waiting until we know more. The U.S. Congress's Office of Technology Assessment concludes that "initial delays of ten or 20 years in implementing emission stabilization will have little effect on ultimate atmospheric carbon concentrations."

Industry has often been accused of wanting to delay all action until the scientific questions are answered, but that's not true. The prestigious Marshall Institute recently released a report unambiguously stating that "no scientific justification now exists for economically punishing policies aimed at global reductions in the emission of carbon dioxide." The report went on to state that "[T]here is time for climatological research in coming years to provide a firmer basis for the consideration of global strategies." These conclusions mirror those of leading academics at institutions like MIT who have been pursuing the climate issue in a rigorous and scholarly manner. The irony is that emerging scientific information has so far reduced the magnitude of the threat, although considerable uncertainties remain.

Yet the political process still pushes the agenda ahead of the science, and advocates remain undaunted. Indeed, as they become more speculative about catastrophe they move further from the science. Instead of adjusting theory and models to the facts, especially those associated with sixteen years of satellite measurements, the advocates deny reality. That's turning the scientific process on its head and it should cause all of us to worry about the unintended consequences of such behavior.

Let me now move to the economic realities.

Economic Realities

Stripped of the rhetoric, the Administration's climate action plan consists of policies that can be implemented without significant economic risks and which make sense on their own merits. If future scientific evidence shows that additional actions are warranted, we will have to face up to that reality. But in the meantime, enlightened self-interest requires that we evaluate the economic implications of the emissions reductions suggested in the Berlin Mandate.

First, the cost of mitigation is a function of time. Reducing emissions over a longer time period will be far less harmful to our economic well-being than forcing rapid reductions. I have no doubt that if we tried to reduce greenhouse gas emissions by 20 percent over the next few years we would bring on a full-scale depression. On the other hand, returning to 1990 levels over a period of several decades might not impose unreasonable economic burdens. So time is important. Accepting this reality helps us better understand the trade-offs worthy of consideration.

And delay will not necessarily increase the costs of mitigation. As new technologies evolve and the state of knowledge improves, emissions reductions will likely cost less. For example, a new power plant using natural gas to produce electricity with combined cycle gas turbine technology will emit only 40 percent of the carbon dioxide emissions of the coal-fired plant it replaces. But transitions require investment capital. And economic growth is needed to generate both capital and technologies. The Office of Technology Assessment concluded that making efficient decisions would save trillions of dollars.

Furthermore, if we squander scarce resources on a global hobgoblin, we will set back efforts to address many real and pressing problems of the developing nations—famine, disease, safe water supplies, and reducing local air pollution.

Planning under uncertainty requires a step-by-step approach. For example, Dr. Alan Manne suggests a "learn-then-act" approach, a rational course of action that reminds me of what former Secretary of Energy Jim Schlesinger once called "Lewis and Clark" planning, named for the explorers. Unlike a Cook's Tour vacation, where every step is laid out in advance and is known with certainty, Lewis and Clark made decisions on which way to go at every fork. With uncertainty, you get where you want to go best by evaluating new information all the time and making decisions along the way.

Given the tremendous uncertainties that lie before us, the Lewis and Clark approach—not the Cook's Tour—is the right paradigm. We can take small steps now and later move at a pace and direction consistent with new knowledge. Dr. Manne of Stanford asserts that even after 2020, enough time would be left to adapt the global economy to a sharp decline in carbon emissions if needed. But forcing abatement now for political reasons—the Cook's Tour approach—would be expensive, inefficient and almost certainly wrong.

A More Rational Approach

Ideally, the political will can be found to fix this international process before we have caused real damage. The . . . scientific and economic realities all point to a different approach. If the global warming threat is to be addressed seriously, all of us need to reject expediency and work towards a process that can be defended on scientific and economic grounds. Here is what I think the broad outlines of a road map for a more rational approach might look like.

First, our political leaders must find a way to redirect what is in fact a badly flawed process. It cannot produce a credible response and our continued support of it will do more harm than good. Future international working group activities have to be organized differently to minimize political gamesmanship and beggar-thy-neighbor policies. A defensible process is needed to create public support for any policies that need to be implemented when, or if, the time comes. In the U.S., for example, tough issues like social security reform and base closings have been handled by commissions to escape an immobilizing political dynamic. It ought to be possible to construct an international analogy that is driven by objectivity, realism, insulated from near-term political needs and reflects energy, finance and trade in addition to environmental considerations.

Second, a plan for providing relevant, timely, peer-reviewed climate research should be the keystone of this effort. Learning from reviews of the NAPAP experience, we are now in a position to coordinate independent research to answer questions in a way that drives the policy-making process. As Lester Lave, a public policy expert from Carnegie Mellon, pointed out, the overall research agenda should address the most important problems, research should be sequenced appropriately, the most cost-effective methods should be used, and unimportant issues should be avoided. In the U.S. we are currently spending about $2 billion annually on global change research. Does anyone really think that we're getting $2 billion in value?

Third, climate change decisions should be driven not by hyperbole and apocalyptic nonsense, but by our best estimate of what the future might actually hold over a time frame that is knowable. Economic analysis should be carefully done with adaptation assessed as part of the equation. Adaptation is not a rubric to skew model results, it is what humans have been doing throughout the millennia in response to almost continuous climate change. We should insist that each step into an uncertain future be guided by well-informed decisions that consider trade-offs and relevant consequences.

And fourth, if emissions are to be reduced, they must be reduced at the least cost to minimize the impact on economic development and world living standards. A key part of this path forward should be joint implementation. It is the best, fastest, least expensive way of addressing emissions where they are growing fastest—in the developing countries. Without joint implementation and appropriate crediting as part of the solution, industrialized countries could spend exorbitant amounts to restrain emissions with hardly any impact on the amount of carbon in the atmosphere. That doesn't make sense.

And last, industry, here and abroad, has tremendous technological resources that can bring innovation to bear on the problem. Technology diffusion can increase efficiency and reduce emissions while boosting economic growth from country to country. If we really want to reduce emissions in the long-term, policies must encourage investment and expand property rights.

Given the potential seriousness of the climate change threat, all of us should be willing to work for a better process. There is no reason on earth why the United States should participate in a process that doesn't serve our self-interest or the self-interest of those who see us as the model for their own aspirations.

"Those who are now seeking to delay the time at which we recognize the connection between the accumulation of greenhouse gases and global climate change are . . . wrong."

Immediate Measures Should Be Taken to Combat Global Warming

Al Gore

Al Gore has served as a senator from Tennessee and as vice president of the United States. He is the author of *Earth in the Balance: Ecology and the Human Spirit*. The following viewpoint is adapted from a speech Gore delivered at George Washington University in Washington, D.C., on March 17, 1995. Gore argues that current measures used to fight global warming do not adequately address the scope of the problem. Unless every nation takes immediate and far-reaching steps to reduce carbon emissions, he asserts, the changes in the Earth's climate will be disastrous.

As you read, consider the following questions:

1. What evidence does the author present to support his contention that global climate change is occurring?
2. Why is the Framework Convention on Climate Change inadequate, in Gore's opinion?
3. In the author's view, who should take the lead in reducing greenhouse gas emissions?

From Al Gore, "Global Climate Change: Protecting the Environment," *U.S. Department of State Dispatch*, April 3, 1995.

Greenhouse gases are building up rapidly in the atmosphere. Concentrations of carbon dioxide have increased about 25% since the Industrial Revolution; nitric oxide has gone up by 15%; methane has gone up by more than 100%.

Change Is Coming

Scientists also agree that continuing this buildup of greenhouse gases will cause the climate to change. The operative word in that sentence is not may, it is will. A continued buildup of this kind will cause the climate to change. About that there is no serious disagreement. The scientific community cannot tell us the pace of these changes or the precise pattern they will take, but they are telling us that change is coming.

There is an international consensus that global surface temperatures could increase from an average of 2°F to 8°F over the next century. That is the rate unseen on this planet for at least the last 10,000 years. That is, unseen during the entire history of human civilization. Since the first cities appeared on the earth, no such change has been seen.

The United States and other areas in high latitudes are projected to warm even more, with increases of up to 10°F. In just the last century, the earth's temperature has risen by about 1°F. The nine warmest years in this century have all occurred since 1980, even though the eruption of Mt. Pinatubo, as predicted at the time, held down temperatures for about three years, until the heavy particulates blocking out a tiny fraction of the sun's radiation fell back out of the atmosphere to earth.

Already, there is ominous evidence of significant change underway. Alpine glaciers in every part of the world are retreating rapidly. You may have seen the pictures not long ago of the prehistoric traveler whose body was found in a mountain pass in the Alps in Italy. They were walking along, and there he was. Why had no one noticed him there for the last 5,000 years? Because the ice covering him has not melted in 5,000 years. It . . . has now melted.

In other areas that have not seen the ice retreat in human experience, it is now retreating. There is a decrease in northern hemisphere snow cover, evidence of a decrease in Arctic sea ice. Average precipitation in the lower 48 states has increased in the last century by about 5%. Torrential rains have increased in the summer during agricultural growing seasons.

These are troubling, complex, and challenging issues to confront, but we should not imagine that they occur according to a pattern of slow and gradual change. We know that natural systems are replete with thresholds beyond which change can occur suddenly and dramatically. A warmer earth alters precipitation, soil moisture, and sea level that can lead to changes in the ideal ranges for crops, forests, and wetlands. Changes in precipitation patterns cause drought in some areas and more rainfall in others. It causes a change in the distribution of microbial populations and vulnerabilities to viruses and bacteria; a change in the distribution of pests; and a change in the distribution of plant and animal life.

Global Warming's Dramatic Effects

Combinations of changes can have dramatic effects—increased rainfall can lead to more floods which together with higher sea levels can threaten the existence of some low-lying coastal communities, and threaten the existence even of some small island nations and low-lying coastal nations.

We have seen concern expressed by scientists in several parts of the world about the increased frequency of drastic weather events. In our own country, we have seen the effects of a shift in the pattern that we call El Nino, from a pattern that occurs every two to five years to a relatively new pattern beginning in the early 1980s in which it has a tendency to become almost constant. . . .

Results of a Wait-and-See Policy

If climate warming is a reality, it might not be that costly to adjust. Why not wait until we have all the answers? Would it not be better to put our efforts into other problems?

The problem is that the cure will be tougher the longer we wait. The authors of the IPCC [Intergovernmental Panel on Climate Change] report provide an illustrative example: In all scenarios, carbon dioxide emissions have to decline in order to achieve stable concentrations at the doubling of carbon dioxide by 2090. If we start in the year 2000, a gradual reduction of 17 percent is sufficient. If measures are not implemented until 2020, however, the model calculates that a reduction of 60 percent (from 2020 levels) is necessary to achieve the targets.

Annika Nilsson, *Greenhouse Earth*, 1992.

In 1993, the Mississippi flooding caused an estimated $10–$20 billion worth of damage. Hurricane Hugo cost the Federal Government alone about $1.6 billion. Hurricane Andrew topped $2 billion in federal disaster payments and cost property insurers at least $16 billion. The floods and mud slides in California have caused over $2 billion in damage already this year.

Does it make sense for us to assume that we need not take action to diminish the chance that an altered climate pattern will lead to an increase in the frequency of severe events of this sort? We ignore these changes at our peril. I mentioned that climate change can cause a shift in the distribution of microbial populations. The range of infectious diseases such as malaria and dengue fever can change significantly.

How should we respond to this kind of threat? The Clinton Administration believes that we must guard against potentially devastating effects, even as we deepen our scientific understanding of these issues through an aggressive research program. This approach is, in fact, analogous to an insurance policy and is not just an abstract notion.

In 1992, we joined the international community in signing the historic Framework Convention on Climate Change. It was the beginning of a process to design a kind of insurance policy. It was a treaty that called on all nations to work together in an unprecedented effort to protect the global environment. Specifically, the industrialized countries were urged to take the lead by stabilizing greenhouse gas emissions to 1990 levels by the year 2000. . . .

Improving the Agreement

We have said since 1994 that we do not believe that the current agreement is adequate. It contains an aim or goal only for the year 2000, and this aim applies only to a limited number of countries. We are now in a situation in which the maximum response that is politically feasible throughout the world still falls short of what is really needed to address the problem. All the nations of the world will need to work together to develop guidance on what steps to take beyond the year 2000. So we must negotiate a new aim for the future.

In view of these limitations and mindful of our responsibility to the future, we are working with other nations to develop a mandate that can be agreed upon in Berlin in 1995 and can set the course for next steps under the treaty. This will require us all to carefully examine what each of us can do to contribute to further reductions in greenhouse gas emissions. Our goal, in other words, in Berlin is to build a foundation and begin momentum.

Just as there are thresholds in the natural climate system, there are also thresholds in the political system. When evidence accumulates to the point where enough people are no longer willing to listen to skeptics that have arguments that are not grounded in the facts, then beyond that threshold the possibilities for significant action improve dramatically. That is why it is important to develop quality research. We have already begun that process here in the United States and that will be a part of the process we will follow in the future.

But now is the time to re-launch negotiations and walk more concretely toward the treaty's objective. Now is the time to establish a new negotiating mandate that will allow us to fulfill our responsibilities to future generations—a mandate that ensures we move forward from the important first steps outlined for the pre-2000 period.

We strongly believe that all nations must participate in this effort. Certainly, industrialized countries who have contributed most of the problem can and should take the lead—and we shall. But we simply cannot ignore the fact that emissions are rising fastest in developing countries, which together now account for almost 50% of all greenhouse gas emissions in the world. We know that industrialized countries have special responsibilities, and we fully support the convention's call for common but differentiated responsibilities. But we very much want the developing nations to join us at the negotiating table so that together we can define these common but differentiated responsibilities in the post-2000 era, not so that alone we can do less, but so that together we can do more—through trade, technology cooperation, and a host of strategies that offer benefits for all nations.

Action Is Needed

We also must do a better job of ensuring that nations are matching rhetoric with reality; that we are accountable for what we say we will do. To date, only a handful of nations have put forward clear, substantive proposals that move them toward the emission reductions they have enunciated. We must be clear: Good intentions and high-flying rhetoric will not come close to helping us meet the very significant challenges inherent in reducing emissions. What is needed and expected under the treaty is concrete action.

In the negotiations that will follow the Berlin meeting, it is imperative that we establish a menu of measures from which to choose strategies for reaching any new aim set for the post-2000 period. Only an analytic phase as part of the negotiating process can provide us with realizable measures and the realistic understanding of what our expectations and goals should be for the future. But the measures selected must truly achieve emissions reductions, and nations must be prepared to show actions and results.

Finally, we believe that the mandate for negotiations should be concluded as rapidly as possible. We believe that an aggressive, ambitious approach, looking at short-term and long-term goals—that is, for the years 2010 and 2020—can be concluded by 1997, when the third conference of the parties will be held. We think this date is a fair one, one that reflects our view of the importance and urgency of the climate change problem and also gives us the lead time to develop and begin to take advantage of new technologies.

On the one hand, we have nations that will be trying to appease strong constituencies in their countries by outbidding the rest of the national community in their pledges to reduce emissions by future actions. But what future generations need is aggressive, measurable, and ambitious actions and not political promises of future actions.

On the other hand, we have political extremists—some of them in our own country—who would have the United States evade and ignore tough issues like global climate change, ozone depletion, or any number of threats to human and environmental health. Far outside the mainstream of scientific consensus, they would deny the existence of the problem and seek to prevent the United States from even acknowledging its concern, even though the actions that we envision are good both for the environment and for the economy.

Scientific Evidence

This is an intellectually, politically, and morally bankrupt position which must be resisted. It is similar to the position that was taken for so long by the tobacco industry in the face of mounting medical and scientific evidence about the connection between smoking and lung cancer. To this day, the precise causal relationship and all the details about exactly how smoking causes lung cancer cannot be established with precision. But the relationship is accepted. It is a medical fact. Yet, for so long, those—some of those with an economic interest in delaying the recognition of that connection—argued implausibly that the scientific evidence was questionable, ought to be ignored, was insufficient upon which to base any conclusions. They were wrong. Those who are now seeking to delay the time at which we recognize the connection between the accumulation of greenhouse gases and global climate change are also wrong. If you think back to the dramatic fires in Kuwait when the oil fields were set ablaze in 1991, all of that carbon pollution put together amounted to less than 1% of what we put into the earth's environment every year. And that amount continues to increase every year.

"The evidence argues that there is no need for urgent action."

Measures to Combat Global Warming Should Be Delayed

Robert C. Balling Jr.

Robert C. Balling Jr. argues in the following viewpoint that taking immediate action to combat global warming will have very little effect on slowing the Earth's warming trend. Moreover, Balling asserts, as the accuracy of global climate models continues to improve, future models are likely to reveal that global warming is not a dire threat. Policy should be based on scientific evidence, he contends, and the evidence shows that immediate action is not required to control global warming. Balling is the director of Arizona State University's Office of Climatology in Tempe and the author of *The Heated Debate: Greenhouse Predictions Versus Climate Reality*.

As you read, consider the following questions:

1. Assuming a business-as-usual global warming rate of 4°C, how much of a difference would Scenario B make on global warming, according to the author?
2. Scenario B policies of a 1°C "business-as-usual" temperature increase will spare the Earth how much warming, in Balling's opinion?
3. According to Balling, how long will it take to detect any climatic difference if measures are taken to combat global warming?

Global warming is almost always presented as an environmental crisis that can be stopped or minimized with appropriate policy actions. Policymakers can debate the impact and the cost-effectiveness of their policies forever, but from a straight climatological perspective, the evidence suggests that realistic policies are likely to have a minimal climatic impact.

Figure 1 was derived directly from the 1990 IPCC [Intergovernmental Panel on Climate Change] report. The uppermost line represents the IPCC "business-as-usual" trend in global temperature to the year 2100. According to that scenario, the earth will warm by approximately 4°C over the natural, background planetary temperature by the end of the next century. If that were to occur, many elements of the greenhouse disaster would become reality. If we adopt IPCC's "Scenario B"—moving to lower carbon-based fuels, achieving large efficiency increases, controlling carbon monoxide, reversing deforestation, and implementing the Montreal Protocol (dealing with chlorofluorocarbon controls) with full participation—the panel projects that the earth would warm according to the line at the bottom of the black area: still nearly 3°C of warming. Scenario B spares the earth very little warming (the black area); by the year 2050, the policies of this IPCC scenario have spared the earth only 0.3°C of warming. These policies do not stop global warming at all; indeed, they barely slow it.

Furthermore, the climatic impact of any policy is directly dependent on the amount of warming predicted over the next century. Figure 1 also shows the impact of the IPCC scenario assuming a business-as-usual 1°C temperature increase, which is much more consistent with the historical record. The Scenario B policies spare the planet less than 0.3°C by the year 2100, and by 2050, they would have spared the earth something near 0.07°C. As scientists lower their estimate of temperature rise for the next century, they also reduce the potential climate impact of any corrective policies. In a very important 1994 study, scientists performed a numerical modeling study and concluded that it will take seventy to one hundred years to detect any climatic difference between the business-as-usual scenario and the most draconian measures proposed by the IPCC.

Must We Act Now?

Many scientists and policymakers continue to argue that we must act immediately to avoid a greenhouse disaster; waiting, they say, is too dangerous given the threat. Several scientists, however, have evaluated the climate difference between acting immediately and waiting a decade or more to implement selected policies. Michael E. Schlesinger and X. Jiang used a numerical model to simulate the impact of realistic policies hypothetically adopted in 1990, and they calculated the global temperature for the middle of the next century. They then simulated the impact of waiting a decade to implement the same policies and found that the temperature of the earth by the middle of the next century was not affected by the delay. Their results, which support the unpopular view that we do not need to rush into policy regarding the greenhouse issue, obviously generated a tremendous debate in the scientific and policy arenas.

Figure 1 Projected Global Warming

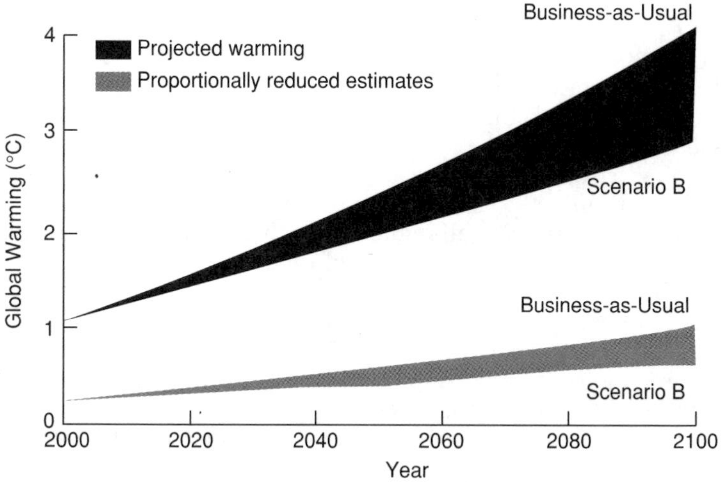

Source: J.T. Houghton, B.A. Callander, and S.K. Varney, eds., *Climate Change 1992: The Supplementary Report to the IPCC Scientific Assessment.*

Nonetheless, many nations seem impatient with the progress made on meeting the many commitments signed at the 1990 Earth Summit in Rio de Janeiro. Accordingly, some nations, including the United States, may be pressured into adopting stronger measures to control greenhouse gas emissions. These measures may increase the costs to the nation and seem doomed to failure. Rather, the evidence argues that there is no need for urgent action, and the suggested measures will probably have only a trivial effect on the global greenhouse gas concentrations.

The Bottom Line

The greenhouse debate will be with us for many years to come. The climate models are getting better all the time, and their predictions for a doubling of atmospheric CO_2 will continue to capture professional and public interest. As the climate effects of other gases are included in the model simulations (e.g., sulfur dioxide), the projected temperature rise will likely be lowered, and the threat of global warming will weaken further. Equally important, climate databases on a variety of variables will continue to be expanded in both time and space. The state-of-the-art satellite-based planetary temperature measurements continue to show no warming at all. As the satellite database grows, I suspect global warming will be even more difficult to prove on empirical grounds. As models and climate databases improve, there is little doubt that the scientists will develop an even better understanding of how the climate system will respond to future changes in atmospheric chemistry.

It seems equally obvious that the greenhouse issue will continue to be a major force in the policy arena. Government agencies, from worldwide to regional organizations, have been developed to deal with the policy concerns raised by the greenhouse issue. Many of these government groups have expanded in recent years, and their very fate is tied to the perception that global warming represents a significant threat to the planet. Bureaucratic inertia virtually guarantees that the greenhouse question will remain high on the list of environmental policy priorities. Despite the evidence, the upcoming versions of the various IPCC reports will continue to trumpet the threat of global warming. Press releases will probably emphasize the risks of the greenhouse effect while remaining silent about the potential benefits of the greenhouse world.

I have become increasingly concerned that a wide gap has opened between many of the policy-oriented groups and the science-oriented groups. Too often policymakers appear to neglect the enormous evidence that argues against the greenhouse disaster and freely accept and promote the scientific evidence in favor of the crisis. It is imperative that the policies developed for the global warming issue be built on the best science available, not on the extreme viewpoints that seem to satisfy and justify the policymakers. The scientific evidence argues against the existence of a greenhouse crisis, against the notion that realistic policies could achieve any meaningful climatic impact, and against the claim that we must act now if we are to reduce the greenhouse threat.

"The [Climate Change Action Plan] will expand markets for important U.S. technologies and services, create jobs in those sectors, and reduce the federal budget deficit."

Measures to Combat Global Warming Are Cost-Effective

Environmental Protection Agency et al.

In October 1993 the Clinton administration released its Climate Change Action Plan, a proposal of 44 recommendations designed to reduce carbon emissions and combat global warming. The following viewpoint is the written testimony of the Environmental Protection Agency, the Department of Energy, the Department of State, and the Council of Economic Advisers that was presented before the House Subcommittee on Health and the Environment. The authors assert that improving energy efficiency is a cost-effective method of reducing carbon emissions. A modest expenditure of government funds will result in substantial private sector investments and reduced energy costs, they contend.

As you read, consider the following questions:

1. In what ways will the Climate Change Action Plan provide economic opportunity in the United States, in the authors' opinion?
2. Projected greenhouse gas emissions must be reduced by how much to return to 1990 levels, according to the authors?

House Committee on Energy and Commerce, Subcommittee on Health and the Environment, *Global Climate Change and Air Pollutants*, 103rd Cong., 1st sess., August 4 and October 26, 1993.

The international scientific community agrees that climate change is the highest risk environmental problem we ultimately face. There is no doubt that human activities are increasing the atmospheric concentrations of greenhouse gases. Theoretical models predict that these increased concentrations will cause changes in regional and global climate systems, which could have serious adverse effects on human health, as well as on ecological and socio-economic systems. While the precise magnitude and patterns of climate change are uncertain, global warming is a growing, long-term threat with profound consequences that would take decades to reverse.

For these reasons, President Bill Clinton committed his Administration to produce a plan to return U.S. greenhouse gas emissions to 1990 levels by the year 2000. The Climate Change Action Plan fulfills that commitment and provides a critical first step in addressing the long-term threat. The Action Plan is the most specific, detailed, and comprehensive plan produced by any nation to date to reduce greenhouse gas emissions. Moreover, the plan demonstrates that there is economic opportunity for the United States in taking on this challenge. The actions detailed in the plan will expand markets for important U.S. technologies and services, create jobs in those sectors, and reduce the federal budget deficit. The plan is good for the global environment, for the U.S. economy, and for the Federal budget.

Development of the Plan

In developing the plan, the Clinton Administration drew on innovative ideas from people in business, labor, government, and the environmental movement. After the President's 1993 Earth Day speech, the White House hosted a Conference on Global Climate Change to explore cost-effective ways of meeting the President's commitment. . . . Prior to the Conference, six working groups were established to identify and analyze specific actions in energy demand, energy supply, transportation, methane and other greenhouse gases, greenhouse gas sinks, and joint implementation. . . .

Two main principles guided the development of the plan as we sought to link the economy to the environment in innovative ways. First, we recognized that achieving the ambitious goal of resuming greenhouse gas emissions to 1990 levels could offer significant economic opportunities—and we were determined to seize these opportunities. Second, the plan was built upon models of successful programs that already exist in the public and private sectors. The programs in the plan are targeted towards proven winners; towards investments in energy efficiency and other technologies which can simultaneously reduce emissions and make the economy more competitive.

Without the Climate Change Action Plan, emissions of the major greenhouse gases (carbon dioxide, methane, nitrous oxides, and hydrofluorocarbons [HFCs]) are projected to grow by about 7 percent between 1990 and 2000, from 1,462 million metric tons of carbon equivalent (MMTCE) to 1,568 MMTCE. Therefore, the policies in the Action Plan must reduce projected U.S. greenhouse gas emissions by about 106 MMTCE in order to meet the goal.

Long-Term Economic Benefits

Many of the programs outlined here will encourage individuals and firms to invest in energy saving equipment or other technologies that yield significant cost savings over the long term. Comparing the magnitude of these investments with the value of energy savings indicates the overall cost-effectiveness of the Climate Change Action Plan. While investing over $60 billion in greenhouse gas emission reductions between 1994 and 2000, individuals and firms realize over $60 billion in energy savings between 1994 and 2000, and realize continued returns in the form of an additional $207 billion in energy savings between 2001 and 2010. By stimulating investments in cost-effective opportunities for greenhouse gas emission reductions, the Action Plan can increase the long-term profits for American business and help consumers save money.

Bill Clinton and Al Gore, *The Climate Change Action Plan*, October 1993.

The plan will attain the emission reduction goal by implementing nearly 50 specific actions that touch every sector of the economy. This is an economy-wide problem that requires economy-wide solutions. The plan accomplishes the goal in a cost-effective manner primarily by harnessing market forces. It leverages a modest government expenditure—about $1.9 billion between 1994 and 2000—which stimulates over $60 billion over the same period in private sector investment in energy efficiency, renewable energy, and other technologies that help reduce greenhouse gas emissions. These investments, in turn, pay substantial dividends to consumers and firms in the form of reduced energy costs—over $60 billion in reduced costs between 1994 and 2000, with continuing cost savings of over $200 billion between 2001 and 2010.

The Action Plan establishes groundbreaking public-private partnerships with key industries across all sectors of the economy to reduce all types of greenhouse gases. For example, the plan contains new agreements with electric utilities to reduce greenhouse gas emissions, as well as agreements with electric motor manufacturers and industrial motor users. Agreements with chemical and aluminum producers will help reduce HFC and PFC emissions. It also includes measures to improve energy efficiency in the commercial, industrial and residential sectors. These energy efficiency improvements are especially cost-effective methods to reduce greenhouse gas emissions—in fact, most of the emission reductions in the plan can be achieved at a profit for U.S. firms and consumers.

Two actions contained in this plan will also help reduce the federal budget deficit. For example, the plan will allow workers the option of taking either employer-paid parking or its cash value as increased income instead—providing a financial incentive to take public transportation or to carpool. While the "cash-out" income would be taxable, new federal revenues would only come from workers who voluntarily chose to exercise their new option. The plan will also give private developers an opportunity to invest in efficiency upgrades at federal hydroelectric dams and market the additional power in exchange for lease and bonus payments.

Building a Healthier Environment

Through this plan, the United States will aggressively promote more recycling, more efficient transportation systems, more reductions in harmful methane emissions from mining and agriculture. The plan protects forest resources that store carbon taken from the atmosphere. The Action Plan contains a pilot project of joint implementation, in order to gain experience in evaluating the emission reduction potential of international investments. The plan will also limit emissions of chlorofluorocarbon substitutes with high global warming potentials. And it establishes a program to monitor the results of the plan and modify it if necessary to adapt to changing circumstances.

Each of the proposed actions is grounded in solid economic analysis. Each will be supported by the funding necessary for effective and rapid implementation. Many of the actions in the plan build upon proven programs and public/private partnerships that can quickly deliver results in order to meet the President's goal.

The Climate Change Action Plan reestablishes the United States as a world leader in protecting the global environment. Hopefully, it will be implemented in concert with other industrial countries as they move to produce their own detailed plans. This plan represents an aggressive first step by the U.S. that will help to build a healthier environment and a stronger economy for decades to come.

> *"The Administration underestimates how much the [Climate Change Action] plan will cost both the government and the private sector, and it overstates projected energy savings."*

Measures to Combat Global Warming Are Not Cost-Effective

John Shanahan

In the following viewpoint, John Shanahan contends that the Clinton Administration's Climate Change Action Plan—a program of 44 initiatives designed to reduce greenhouse gas emissions—is not cost-effective. The administration's estimates of the financial costs and energy savings of the plan are misleading because the costs are underestimated and the benefits are overestimated, Shanahan argues. Many of the plan's initiatives are uneconomical and would hurt businesses, he asserts, while providing few environmental benefits. Shanahan is a policy analyst for the Heritage Foundation, a conservative public policy research organization.

As you read, consider the following questions:

1. What are some of the ways the Climate Change Action Plan purports to reduce greenhouse gas emissions, according to the author?
2. In what way were the costs of the Climate Change Action Plan's underestimated, in Shanahan's opinion?

Excerpted from John Shanahan, "Clinton's 'Voluntary' Global Warming Plan: Expensive, Ineffective, and Unnecessary," Heritage Foundation *Backgrounder*, August 3, 1994. Reprinted by permission of The Heritage Foundation, ©1994.

The Administration in Spring 1994 released additional information on President Bill Clinton's "voluntary" 44-point plan to reduce greenhouse gas emissions in the United States to 1990 levels by the year 2000. This plan is designed to address the potential threat of global warming, or the enhanced greenhouse effect, which is the unproved theory that man-made emissions will raise the temperature of the Earth's atmosphere. The President's plan, as outlined, would be a mistake for the United States and should be reviewed carefully by Congress, the media, and the public.

The Administration's calculation of costs and benefits is flawed [because] the plan would impose more than $60 billion of unnecessary costs on the economy over six years. . . .

The Clinton Plan

The Climate Change Action Plan to reduce greenhouse gases was announced by President Bill Clinton in October 1993, and an explanatory supplement was released in late March 1994. The plan is to form the cornerstone of the U.S. commitment to the international Framework Convention on Climate Change. This international agreement, which requires that a National Action Plan be developed and submitted, was signed by President George Bush in June 1992 and became effective in 1994. It requires that countries reduce greenhouse gas emissions eventually to 1990 levels and that some progress be made by the year 2000. But President Clinton has pledged his commitment that the United States will attain the full 1990 levels by the year 2000.

The plan is a potpourri of initiatives designed primarily to encourage companies and households—by persuasion, by education, and in some instances by compulsion—to reduce greenhouse gas emissions, such as carbon dioxide and methane, produced in the manufacture or use of a product. This would be accomplished by such means as reducing energy consumption (which produces greenhouse gases) and limiting methane releases from garbage dumps or landfills. In all, the plan has 44 different initiatives ranging from mandates that household appliances and buildings be made more energy-efficient to increased government funding of the Green Lights Program, an educational program created during the Bush Administration to show companies how they can reduce energy consumption while saving money. Other initiatives, such as the Source Reduction, Pollution Reduction, and Recycling Initiative, focus on spending federal monies to persuade companies to reduce their emissions voluntarily without legislative mandates. Yet another initiative is designed to reduce cow flatulence through improved techniques of beef production. The Clinton Administration's plan relies in part on existing legislative authority to implement the initiatives through regulatory action, but it would also require significant additional federal spending.

How the Costs Are Underestimated

The Clinton Administration estimates that it will cost $63.4 billion to implement this plan through the year 2000. Of this amount, the private sector's share is $61.5 billion, the government's only $1.9 billion. Most of the public sector funds, it is claimed, will be transferred from other funding sources. At the same time, the Administration projects savings to the economy of $268.1 billion, primarily in energy savings if the initiatives are implemented.

Unfortunately, the Administration's figures are highly misleading. Specifically, the Administration underestimates how much the plan will cost both the government and the private sector, and it overstates projected energy savings by using flawed accounting procedures and unduly optimistic forecasts. Experience teaches that once government programs are born, they almost never die, yet the Administration assumes that every government program initiated or augmented by the plan will cease within seven years. It also assumes that all private sector costs will drop to zero at that time. Thus, although these programs will continue to exist, and will probably grow, the Administration ignores all costs that will be incurred after the year 2000 and implicitly assumes that the costs of maintaining greenhouse gas emissions at 1990 levels will be zero—while calculating the benefits from energy savings derived from the plan until the year 2010, or for 17 years, with benefits beyond the year 2000 included in the calculation of costs and benefits. Moreover, while it is true that some costs borne in the early years will continue to reap benefits for another decade, this is not true of all programs.

This disparity in the calculation of costs and benefits is only one way in which the Administration distorts the plan's true costs and savings. Another is its highly unusual accounting method. Under the standard method, future figures would be discounted to their present value; the Administration, however, has chosen to calculate all cost and benefit figures in undiscounted 1991 dollars. The result: the plan's supposed benefits are inflated far more than its costs because cost or benefit figures occurring further in the future are inflated proportionately more. Thus, potential but undiscounted savings yielded 17 years from now are greatly inflated, while costs 7 years from now are only somewhat exaggerated. This deliberate obfuscation of the real costs and benefits indicates that the Administration knows the real present value costs of its program exceed the real benefits discounted for inflation and the time value of money. If the

Administration truly believes the benefits justify the costs, it should present real figures calculated in the standard way.

Even using this flawed accounting methodology, the Administration significantly underestimates the probable costs and overestimates the likely benefits of many of the plan's initiatives. Perhaps the best example is Action #16—the source reduction, pollution prevention, and recycling program—which encourages and subsidizes increased recycling of, and reduced use in products and packaging of, certain natural resources such as paper, plastic, and other materials. The plan estimates this program will cost the government and private sector $176 million but save the economy $36.5 billion, or 207 times as much. If such a generous return on an investment was possible, it seems odd that entrepreneurs would have not already seized the opportunity without the need for government encouragement. In reality, however, recycling is expensive and generally uneconomical, with the exception of aluminum found in such products as cans. Thus, the cost for the private sector will be much higher than the Administration forecasts, and benefits that otherwise might offset these costs will be lower.

Passing on the Costs to Employees and Consumers

One of the most costly aspects will be the move to encourage mass transit. As usual, the disappointing performance of publicly owned mass transit systems is blamed on a lack of sufficient funding and the "subsidy" given to workers in the form of "free" parking. The tax code will be altered to treat parking spaces as personal income, to the tune of $2.2 billion in new federal revenues.

Although not stressed in the initial coverage, household appliances will be required to achieve higher levels of energy efficiency, raising the price of home air conditioners, water heaters, stoves and even television sets.

Kent Jeffreys, *Wall Street Journal*, October 22, 1993.

Similarly, redesigning packaging and other products to reduce their natural resources content is very expensive. Past trends indicate that manufacturers already try to cut packaging costs because packaging, which adds weight and volume to a product, is expensive to buy, store, and transport. Expensive government programs to encourage less packaging are thus unnecessary. At worst, they can be counterproductive by encouraging manufacturers to reduce packaging when it is uneconomical. For instance, reducing paper packaging of food can be counterproductive because every pound of paper packaging reduces food waste by an average of 1.41 pounds. Thus, reductions would waste valuable food while increasing total garbage destined for landfills.

The Administration also obscures the true cost of reducing greenhouse gases by not counting funds dedicated to efforts now underway, or programs already announced, that comprise part of the plan. In short, $63 billion is not the total amount to be spent on reducing greenhouse gases; it is only the additional amount to be dedicated to this effort. One cannot accurately gauge the true costs either to the government or to the private sector until the White House is more candid in estimating how much is now being spent to fight global warming and combining that with accurate, discounted, and itemized projections as to how much its new initiatives will cost Americans. . . .

The Plan Squanders Money

Faced with an uncertain science and the known consequences of rash action, sound public policy demands that lawmakers use care in choosing how the United States addresses global warming. If billions of dollars are squandered on what turns out to be a "Chicken Little" threat, lawmakers will have failed in their duty.

As envisioned, the Clinton Administration's National Action Plan will impose large costs on all households even though scientists remain divided as to whether adverse climate changes will occur. The wisest course of action would be to increase the corpus of knowledge of the Earth's atmosphere before spending billions on potentially unnecessary programs.

Periodical Bibliography

The following articles have been selected to supplement the diverse views presented in this chapter. Addresses are provided for periodicals not indexed in the *Readers' Guide to Periodical Literature*, the *Alternative Press Index*, or the *Social Sciences Index*.

Laura Alderson	"Global Climate Change: Turning the Tide," *Environmental Health Perspective*, May 1994. Available from Superintendent of Documents, PO Box 371954, Pittsburgh, PA 15250-7954.
Kenneth Neill Cameron	"Atmospheric Destruction and Human Survival," *Political Affairs*, January 1993.
Milton R. Copulos	"Global Warming Warning: Not Just for Rich Nations," *Christian Science Monitor*, September 20, 1993.
Tori DeAngelis	"Spheres of Influence: Clinton's Climate Change Action Plan," *Environmental Health Perspective*, May 1994.
Philip Elmer-Dewitt	"Not Just Hot Air," *Time*, May 3, 1993.
Robert D. Glasser and Michael A. Cohen	"Funds Cool, Earth Keeps Warming," *Christian Science Monitor*, July 25, 1995.
Mark Hertsgaard	"Global Warning," *New York Times*, April 8, 1995.
Michael D. Lemonick	"Stop Polluting, Please," *Time*, November 1, 1993.
Michael Mautner	"Engineering Earth's Climate from Space," *Futurist*, March/April 1993.
David Malin Roodman	"Pioneering Greenhouse Policy," *World Watch*, July/August 1993. Available from PO Box 6991, Syracuse, NY 13217-9942.
S. Fred Singer	"White House Zealots Skirt Scientific Truth About Warming," *Insight*, September 13, 1993. Available from 3600 New York Ave. NE, Washington, DC 20002.
Peter N. Spotts	"New Global Warming Report: Don't Panic, but Let's Take Action," *Christian Science Monitor*, December 18, 1995.
William K. Stevens	"Nations to Consider Toughening Curbs on Global Warming," *New York Times*, February 21, 1995.
William K. Stevens	"Price of Global Warming? Debate Weighs Dollars and Cents," *New York Times*, October 10, 1995.
USA Today	"Trees Can Slow the Greenhouse Effect," June 1994.

How Can the Rain Forests Be Preserved?

GLOBAL
WARMING

Chapter Preface

A number of scientists and environmentalists who are concerned about global warming have focused their attention on preserving the world's rain forests. These researchers believe that carbon dioxide is a major contributor to global warming. By removing carbon dioxide from the atmosphere during the photosynthesis process, advocates contend, rain forests help to minimize increases in climatic temperatures. Because the forests provide this natural defense against global warming, many scientists argue, efforts to conserve them are crucial.

Plans to save the forests have met with two primary obstacles. One obstacle is presented by residents of less developed nations who live in the rain forests and who contend that they have the right to use the rain forests in order to survive. They argue that they need the money that they receive from selling rain forest timber or from raising cattle in areas where the forests have been cleared. The second obstacle comes from economists and other critics who maintain that the market should determine the use of resources—in this case, the rain forests. As long as there is a market for tropical timber or for beef cattle, they contend, rain forest preservation must be secondary to economic interests.

As a result, many scientists and environmentalists have looked for alternatives to raising cattle or selling timber that will preserve the rain forests, ensure local residents' survival, and also satisfy market forces. They have implemented a host of programs designed to persuade the world that the rain forests are more valuable standing than cut. According to George M. Woodwell and Kilparti Ramakrishna of the Woods Hole Research Center, "Letting the forests die is self-destructive. Their role as a filter of the world's pollution, a sponge that absorbs carbon dioxide and slows global warming, is crucial to the life of the earth." The viewpoints in the following chapter present a variety of options designed to preserve the rain forests.

"Institutional reforms in the forestry sector . . . are . . . needed to help save the world's remaining tropical forests."

Improved International Initiatives Can Help Preserve the Rain Forests

Anjali Acharya

As concern rose over the clearing of the tropical rain forests the international community responded with treaties and plans designed to stop the destruction. In the following viewpoint, Anjali Acharya contends that these treaties have largely failed to stop rain forest destruction. She argues that the international community should strengthen these initiatives and add others in order to protect the forests. Acharya is on the staff of the Worldwatch Institute, an environmental protection and watchdog organization in Washington, D.C.

As you read, consider the following questions:

1. According to Acharya, what are the primary causes of deforestation in different parts of the world?
2. How has the destruction of tropical forests affected plant and animal species, according to the author?
3. What is the effect of rain forest destruction on climate, according to Acharya?

Anjali Acharya, "Tropical Forests Vanishing," in *Vital Signs 1995*, edited by Linda Clarke, (New York: W.W. Norton, 1995). Copyright © 1995 by Worldwatch Institute. Reprinted by permission. Footnotes in the original have been omitted here.

Over the years, tropical forests have been extensively cleared to extract timber, build cattle ranches, grow crops, and construct dams and highways. During the eighties alone, the world lost about 8 percent of its tropical forests—a decline from 1,910 million hectares in 1980 to 1,756 million hectares in 1990. This widespread deforestation is driving countless species to extinction, threatening indigenous cultures and the livelihoods of millions of people, and affecting local and global climate.

Climate Regulation

Tropical forests account for a third of the world's forests and contain about four-fifths of the world's land vegetation—ranging from constantly wet rain forests to dry thorn woodlands. Covering less than 12 percent of the earth's land surface, these forests provide habitat for 50–90 percent of the world's species, and are home to millions of communities that depend on them. They play a vital role in climate regulation by storing carbon that would have otherwise been released to the atmosphere. Tropical forests provide about a fifth of all wood used worldwide in industry. A quarter of the world's pharmaceutical drugs use rain forest plant extracts as ingredients.

Rain forests, in particular, support an incredible diversity of species—providing habitat to more than 60 percent of all known species of plants, 40 percent of birds of prey, and as many as 80 percent of all known insects. The profusion of species in these forests, many of which are found nowhere else, is unequaled by any other biome. Ecuador, for example, is roughly the same size as the United Kingdom but has almost seven times the number of bird species—1,435 species compared with 219.

In the eighties, tropical forests were cleared at an average annual rate of 15.4 million hectares, almost twice the size of Austria. The Asia and Pacific region had the highest average annual deforestation rate (1.2 percent), followed by Latin America and the Caribbean (0.8 percent) and Africa (0.7 percent).

Causes of Deforestation

The primary causes of deforestation vary. Asian forests are threatened by commercial logging and agricultural expansion, while the main pressures in Africa include fuelwood collection, overgrazing of cattle, and logging. In Latin America, forest clearance is usually associated with cattle ranching, population resettlement schemes, and major development projects, with some commercial logging.

Logging remains one of the major driving forces behind the loss of tropical forest. Timber harvesting usually involves building a dense network of roads, which exposes forests to exotic pests and diseases, increases soil erosion, and opens up previously inaccessible forests to miners, ranchers, and poor farmers.

To feed the world's growing timber demand, there has been a consistent rise in both total area logged as well as volume of wood produced each year from tropical forests. Globally, 5.9 million hectares are logged annually in the tropics, including 4.9 million hectares in primary forests. Today, tropical forests supply about 30 percent of the world's log exports, 12 percent of sawnwood exports, and 60 percent of plywood and veneer exports. Nearly half comes from Southeast Asia.

Forest Cover by Region, 1990, and Annual Deforestation, 1981–90

Region	Forest Cover 1990	Annual Deforestation, 1981–90	
	(mill. hectares)		(percent)
Asia and the Pacific	310.6	3.9	1.2
Latin America and Caribbean	918.1	7.4	0.8
Africa	527.6	15.4	0.8
Total	1,756.3	15.4	0.8

Source: U.N. Food and Agriculture Organization, *Forest Resources Assessment 1990: Tropical Countries*.

Megadevelopment projects, such as hydroelectric dams and highways, are also opening up previously impenetrable areas of forests to settlers. In the Amazonian state of Rondônia, the construction of the BR-364 road, accompanied by the chaotic infusion of settlers, led to a drop in forest cover from 97 percent in 1980 to 76 percent in 1990.

Shifting cultivation, which involves burning and cutting down forests to grow crops, becomes unsustainable under conditions of poverty, population pressure, and unequal land-ownership. Population resettlement schemes in Indonesia and Brazil have encouraged people to settle on forestland, which has subsequently been converted to cropland. As much as 5 million hectares of tropical forests are destroyed every year by poor landless peasants. Today, Indonesia's rain forests are being cleared for cultivation at a rate of around 200,000 hectares each year.

The Effects of Cattle Ranching

Since the mid-1970s, cattle ranches have replaced tropical forests on more than 20 million hectares in Latin America. Two-thirds of forest destruction in Costa Rica is attributed to cattle ranching. In Central and South America, about 2 million hectares of forest land is cleared every year to create cattle pasture.

Such deforestation, along with fragmentation and degradation of tropical forests, is leading to devastating losses of plant and animal species. In particular, species-rich rain forests are being reduced by 4.6 million hectares annually. Harvard biologist E.O. Wilson estimates that in tropical rain forests alone, roughly 50,000 species a year—nearly 140 each day—are either extinguished or condemned to eventual extinction by the destruction of their habitat. At current deforestation rates, the earth may lose about 25 percent of its species by the middle of the twenty-first century.

The millions of indigenous people who live within tropical rain forests are threatened as well. Africa's last rain forest people, the Pygmies, are threatened by rapidly shrinking forests, and logging activities in Malaysia's Sarawak state endanger the livelihood and culture of the Penans living there.

The burning and destruction of tropical forests has serious implications for both local and global climate. Extensive forest loss results locally in higher temperatures and lower rainfall, leading to more frequent and serious droughts. Global loss of carbon from deforestation in tropical countries is estimated at 1.1–3.6 billion tons—about 30 percent of total carbon emissions.

International Initiatives

In the past, international forestry initiatives such as the Tropical Forestry Action Plan, the International Tropical Timber Agreement, and the U.N. Statement of Forest Principles have failed to check forest loss. New and strengthened efforts are now needed to arrest tropical deforestation. These should include improved protection and conservation measures, restricted trade in threatened timber species and widespread adoption of sustainable forestry practices. Institutional reforms in the forestry sector, accompanied by restructured tenure and forest product pricing policies, are also needed to help save the world's remaining tropical forests.

"Scenes [from] Vancouver Island's western shore have spawned a worldwide campaign to save what remains of British Columbia's temperate rain forest."

Political Pressure Can Help Preserve the Rain Forests

Mark Clayton

In the following viewpoint, Mark Clayton asserts that local and international political pressure has forced the provincial government of British Columbia to enact measures to preserve its temperate rain forests. He contends that environmentalists from Canada and other countries have pressured businesses and the international community to reduce their use of Canadian wood products in order to force changes in logging practices. Clayton is a staff writer for the *Christian Science Monitor*, an international daily newspaper.

As you read, consider the following questions:

1. According to Clayton, why has British Columbia been nicknamed "the Brazil of the North"?
2. What role did Greenpeace play in preserving Clayoquot Sound's forests, according to the author?
3. What specific measures did the government pass, according to Clayton, to help preserve the forests?

The mountain was once covered with ancient rain forest. Now many locals refer to it as Kojak after the bald-headed television character.

Scenes like this one on Vancouver Island's western shore have spawned a worldwide campaign to save what remains of British Columbia's temperate rain forest.

A Major Victory

Environmentalists won a major victory toward that end on July 6, 1995, when the province's government approved wholesale reforms of logging practices in the area that has become the center of the controversy—Clayoquot Sound.

"There's no question Clayoquot has a symbolic power globally," says Jerry Franklin, a forestry expert from Seattle's University of Washington who sat on the scientific panel that recommended the reforms.

The new practices will not end logging, but the rate of cut appears sure to slow dramatically in an effort to protect the forest's biodiversity, ranging from rare plants and animals to salmon-bearing streams and microorganisms in the soil.

But there are already signs that the battle over Canadian forests is far from over. Sharon Chow of the Sierra Club of Western Canada says greater protection of Clayoquot Sound, though a big step forward, is not enough.

"We have to apply this technique to the whole of British Columbia," she says. Green groups have dubbed the province "the Brazil of the North" because of it's comparable rate of deforestation—75 million cubic meters of wood annually. (Clayoquot Sound represents less than 3 percent of that.) The province's major forest-products firms, such as MacMillan Bloedel Ltd., insist that the new practices were designed specifically for Clayoquot Sound and are not intended to spread provincewide.

Protests Continue

Even in the sound, conflict may be brewing again. Valerie Langer, leader of the Friends of Clayoquot Sound, says "we might be blockading" if negotiations with MacMillan Bloedel fail to stop the company from logging in Shark Creek. Ms. Langer says the company should voluntarily withdraw from the area because of the government's decision. More broadly, she adds, if the new guidelines are not implemented, blockades could follow.

The prospect of more protests is frustrating to many local residents, who have grown tired of the tension between loggers and conservationists. Major standoffs with timber companies occurred in 1984 and in 1993, when protesters were arrested for sitting on an active logging road.

Gary Patrucco, a forester in MacMillan Bloedel's Clayoquot Sound branch, says he is growing tired of being constantly "under the gun" from environmentalists.

Source: *Christian Science Monitor.*

He notes that significant changes had been made before the government's adoption of the practices recommended by a scientific panel commissioned two years ago to come up with a plan for the sound. The industry's current maximum size for clear-cuts is 100 acres—far smaller than "Kojak." And a new provincewide forest-practices code strengthens protection for streams.

Some Loggers Are Sympathetic

Looking over a small clear-cut from atop a pile of slash, logger Bill Critchlow says, "In 10 years time, it'll look like that piece up there." He points to a hillside covered by young green trees.

The MacMillan Bloedel worker sees a dialogue with the green groups as healthy. "They do have some valid points. The companies have been getting their way for too long," he says. The current situation is an industry "opportunity . . . to grow beyond the old image" of carelessness. But in the end, Mr. Critchlow worries that critics "live in a dream world," ignoring logging's important role in the province's economy.

"Who's going to pay for all of this [reduction in cutting]?" he asks.

The provincial government is projecting that new practices will be more labor-intensive, so that a lower rate of cut need not mean fewer jobs. The companies logging the sound (MacMillan Bloedel and International Forest Products Ltd., known as Interfor) have pledged to retain current employment levels.

Saving Trees Benefits Tourism

Environmentalists, meanwhile, argue that tourism—already the province's largest employer with 105,000 jobs in 1993—can only thrive if beautiful scenery is preserved.

Their main argument, however, is over biodiversity, not aesthetics. Second-growth forests (what grows back after cutting) are inferior as wildlife habitat and will have less genetic diversity than old-growth forests, environmentalists argue.

Most of the world's original temperate rain forest has already been cut. Most of what remains is in Alaska and British Columbia, and is being logged rapidly.

Europeans Are Watching

"A lot of people in Europe, one of Canada's main markets, are watching what happens here very closely," says Mr. Franklin of the University of Washington.

In 1994 Greenpeace International conducted an intense campaign directed at European consumers of British Columbia pulp and paper. Environmentalists dramatized their point by dragging along a flatbed trailer with a huge red-cedar stump from Clayoquot called "Stumpie."

In Britain, threats of consumer boycotts have already led the British subsidiary of Scott Paper Company to cancel a $5 million contract with MacMillan Bloedel.

In the United States, Greenpeace and other groups have taken aim at consumers in the publishing industry, including the *New York Times* and telephone-directory makers GTE and the Pacific Telesis Group. Such pressure on the financial bottom line may explain the muted public reaction from companies affected by the adoption of the panel's 120 recommendations.

"We intend to meet the challenge" of the new standards, said Bob Findlay, MacMillan Bloedel's chief executive officer, after the government's decision. The new practices offer hope to the logging companies that the environmental-boycott push will end. But green groups are likely to keep the tool in their arsenal.

"It's not government pressure keeping these companies at the table discussing these issues. It's financial pressure," says Vicky Husband of the Sierra Club of Western Canada.

Political pressure also has played a big role in Clayoquot Sound, others say. Marilyn Burgoon of the Western Canada Wilderness Committee says she remembers well the provincial political impact of the "Clayoquot summer" of 1993, when her 18-year-old-daughter, Vanessa, was among the arrested blockaders. It was those arrests, Ms. Burgoon says, that caused the government to appoint the panel, whose report has "vindicated" the protesters. . . .

Strict Restrictions

Key panel recommendations adopted include:

- A planning process focused on which trees should be retained, rather than which will be removed. Site-specific recommendations will take into account biodiversity requirements.
- No logging in pristine watersheds until scientific assessments have been made.
- Restrictions on road construction and stronger protection for streams.
- An expanded role for native tribes in managing forests. Indians make up half the sound's population but currently control only 4 percent of the land.

"With pressures mounting to harvest or clear the remaining temperate rain forest, conserving what survives has become imperative."

Regulating Logging Can Help Preserve the Rain Forests

Derek Denniston

Derek Denniston is on the staff of the Worldwatch Institute, an environmental protection and watchdog organization in Washington, D.C. In the following viewpoint, Denniston asserts that while much media and policy attention has focused on preserving tropical rain forests, the temperate rain forests are in even more danger of destruction. Temperate forests have been heavily logged because of the value of certain kinds of wood, Denniston contends. Only through intense conservation projects and strict restrictions on logging, he argues, will the remaining temperate forests be preserved.

As you read, consider the following questions:

1. What features do all coastal temperate rain forests share, according to Denniston?
2. According to the author, what varieties of trees are particularly valuable?
3. What two reasons does the author give for saving the rain forests?

Derek Denniston, "Conserving the Other Rain Forest," in *Vital Signs 1994*, edited by Linda Clarke, (New York: W.W. Norton, 1995). Copyright ©1994 by Worldwatch Institute. Reprinted by permission. Footnotes in the original have been omitted here.

Although efforts to save the world's tropical rain forests have rightly received widespread attention, another type of rain forest is perhaps even more threatened. Now estimated to cover less than half their original area, coastal temperate rain forests are an exceptionally productive and biologically diverse ecosystem. They include some of the oldest and most massive tree species in the world, and constitute some of the largest remaining pristine landscapes in the temperate zone.

Coastal Temperate Rain Forests

Forest ecologists have found that three physical features are common to all coastal temperate rain forests: proximity to the ocean, the presence of mountains, and, as a result of the atmospheric interaction between the two, high rainfall throughout the year. Thus these forests are distinguished by complex interactions between terrestrial, freshwater, estuarine, and marine ecosystems—especially through the cycling of water.

Coastal temperate rain forests once covered 30–40 million hectares, an area roughly the size of Germany, or less than 0.3 percent of the earth's land area. Since temperate forests now encompass about 2 billion hectares, the coastal rain forest type has always been rare. It existed originally on the western margins of North America, New Zealand, Tasmania, Chile, Argentina, the Black Sea coast of Turkey and Georgia, Norway, Scotland, Ireland, and Iceland.

A preliminary study by Ecotrust and Conservation International estimates that at least 55 percent of the world's coastal temperate rain forest has been logged or cleared for other uses. The remaining area now spans about 14 million hectares, smaller than the state of Wisconsin.

North America harbors the largest contiguous zone of this type of forest, stretching about 3,000 kilometers from the Alaska Peninsula south through British Columbia and Washington state to Oregon's Siuslaw River. In the southern hemisphere, Chile holds the largest zone, extending from Arauco south into Magellanes province. On Tasmania, broad-leaved temperate rain forest has provided refuge for some of the oldest flora in Australia. New Zealand's South Island also hosts a sizable area. In Europe, more than 99 percent of this forest has been cleared or converted into managed forests.

University of Montana forest ecologist Paul Alaback has used the type, amount, and annual distribution of precipitation as well as a critical maximum summer temperature to classify three temperate rain forest types: seasonal, perhumid, and subpolar. He defines temperate rain forests as ecologically distinguished by year-round precipitation that keeps them wet, such that the plant organisms are not adapted to drought and do not naturally burn. Together, the absence of drought, rareness of fire, and cool summers generally distinguish temperate rain forests from all other temperate forests.

Overabundant Precipitation Is Characteristic

Because of the maritime climatic influence, overabundant precipitation falls virtually year-round—often in the form of fog, drizzle, and light rain. Thus temperate rain forests have little variation in temperature, adding to the fertile growing conditions. The heavy rainfall and low temperatures also combine to produce some of the highest runoff rates in the temperate zone, leading to rapid rock weathering and soil formation, as well as frequent landslides and other forms of erosion. Complex riparian networks add to the structural diversity of the forest. Together with frequent coastal winds, these processes make temperate rain forests one of the most dynamic and productive ecosystems on earth.

Status of Unlogged and Protected Coastal Temperate Rain Forest

Region	Unlogged	Protected[1]
	(percent)	
Alaska	89	36
Argentina	?	?
British Columbia	43	5?
Chile	40	7?
Europe[2]	<1	0
New Zealand	28	28
Oregon	4	2
Tasmania	85	60
Washington	25	21
Total	45	17

[1]Figures for protected areas are inflated due to the inclusion of unforested, alpine areas. [2]Includes Iceland, Norway, Ireland, Scotland, Georgia, and Turkey.

Source: Erin Kellogg, ed., "Coastal Temperate Rain Forests: Ecological Characteristics, Status and Distribution Worldwide" (a working manuscript), Occasional Paper Series No. 1, Ecotrust/Conservation International, Portland, Ore., June 1992.

No other terrestrial ecosystem produces as much living matter (biomass) per unit of area—as much as 500–2,000 tons per hectare (compared with about 100 in tropical rain forests). Not surprisingly, coastal temperate rain forests host some of the oldest, largest trees in the world—such as an ancient Sitka spruce more than 95 meters tall and 3 meters thick at its base in the Carmanah Valley on Vancouver Island in British Columbia. Indices for the biological diversity of lichen and bryophytes (mosses and liverworts) in these forests may be comparable with those of tropical rain forests. Providing a steady supply of dissolved nutrients, particulate organic matter, and large woody debris, these forests also help sustain some of the world's most productive shellfish beds and spawning grounds for commercially valued fish species.

The global demand for the wood products of these forests has been the primary force driving their loss. Among the most valuable timber species are South America's alerce and monkey puzzle and North America's Sitka spruce, yellow cypress (cedar), and Douglas fir. Temperate rain forests have evolved and adapted to small-scale disturbances like erosion, landslides, and windthrows (a few trees blown over at a time). But large clear-cuts—virtually the only logging method used in North America—dramatically impair the ecological integrity of these complex, ancient forests.

In Washington and Oregon, temperate rain forests have been harvested for more than a century, leaving only one entire large watershed unlogged. Since 1950, more than half of the most productive rain forest in Alaska's Tongass National Forest has been clear-cut. In Chile and New Zealand, much of the drier hardwood forests have been converted to exotic pine plantations. In Chile, much of the remaining rain forest is increasingly threatened by Japanese and other multinational companies seeking trees for pulping.

On Vancouver Island, logging companies have already removed two-thirds of the original ancient groves; most of what remains is fragmented or clinging to steep slopes, where road building and logging cause erosion, landslides, damage to fish-bearing streams, and soil degradation. In the largest civil disobedience action in Canadian history, more than 850 protesters have been arrested since the summer of 1993 trying to halt logging in Vancouver Island's Clayoquot Sound. Clayoquot's 4,000 square kilometers of interconnected marine, estuarine, and terrestrial ecosystems support abundant fish, seabirds, marine mammals, migratory waterfowl, and more than 100,000 shorebirds—as well as large predators, such as bears, cougars, and Orca whales.

Protecting Forests

Protecting what remains of the world's coastal temperate rain forests will give scientists time to better understand the close relationships between wildlife and forests at the landscape scale. The prospect of global climate change further underlines the need for comparative data on ecosystem processes along analogous climatic gradients, especially at the high latitudes—where the most pronounced changes are expected to occur.

The time is short to continue identifying threatened areas, launch local conservation projects, and perform long-term monitoring and research on local, regional, and global levels. With pressures mounting to harvest or clear the remaining temperate rain forest, conserving what survives has become imperative.

"Environmental entrepreneurs can create commercial alternatives to the traditional damaging uses of rain forest resources."

Sustainable Development Can Help Preserve the Rain Forests

Thomas A. Carr, Heather L. Pedersen, and Sunder Ramaswamy

Development programs that promote the sale of rain forest products help provide financial incentives to local residents to prevent destruction of the forests, the authors argue in the following viewpoint. Programs such as these are called sustainable development because they generate income for local residents and preserve natural resources at the same time. Thomas A. Carr and Sunder Ramaswamy are assistant professors of economics at Middlebury College in Vermont. Heather L. Pedersen teaches mathematics at the Colorado Springs School in Colorado.

As you read, consider the following questions:

1. How much rain forest is lost each year, according to the authors?
2. In the authors' opinion, what are the benefits of sustainable development projects?
3. How does the Tagua Initiative cited by the authors work and how does it help preserve the rain forests?

Excerpted from Thomas A. Carr, Heather L. Pedersen, and Sunder Ramaswamy, "Rain Forest Entrepreneurs," *Environment*, vol. 35, no. 7, September 1993. Reprinted with permission of the Helen Dwight Reid Educational Foundation. Published by Heldref Publications, 1319 18th St. NW, Washington, DC 20036-1802. Copyright ©1993.

Each year, nearly 17 million hectares of rain forest—an area roughly equal to that of Wisconsin—are lost world-wide as a result of deforestation. Because more than half of all species on the planet are found in rain forests, this destruction portends serious environmental consequences, including the decimation of biological diversity. Another threat lies in the fact that rain forests serve as an important sink for carbon dioxide, a greenhouse gas that contributes to global warming. The Amazon region alone stores at least 75 billion tons of carbon in its trees. Furthermore, when stripped of trees, rain forest land soon becomes inhospitable and nonarable because the soil is nutrient-poor and ill-suited to agriculture. Under current practices, therefore, the forests are being destroyed permanently.

Exploiting Rain Forests

Economic forces result in exploitation of the rain forest to extract hardwood timber and fuel and in clearcutting the land for agriculture and cattle ranching, which are primary causes of the devastation. Mounting evidence shows that these conventional commercial and industrial uses of the rain forest are not only ecologically devastating but also economically unsound. These findings have inspired an innovative approach to save the rain forest. Environmental groups are now targeting their efforts toward developing commercially viable and sustainable uses of the rain forest. Their strategy is to create economic incentives that encourage local inhabitants to practice efficient stewardship over the standing forests. These environmental entrepreneurs no longer view the market as their nemesis but as an instrument to bring about constructive social and environmental change. In theory, the strategy promotes win-win solutions: Environmentalists gain by preserving the rain forests, and local inhabitants gain from an improved standard of living that is generated by enlightened, sustainable development. In practice, the challenge lies in implementing such programs. . . .

Responding to Deforestation

Although people everywhere may benefit from preserving the rain forest, the costs of preservation are borne mainly by the local inhabitants. Usually, the inhabitants' immediate financial needs far outweigh the long-term benefit gained by foregoing the traditional extractive methods of forestry or land conversion for agriculture. In many of these countries, high levels of poverty, rapid population growth, and unequal distribution of land encourage migration into the forest regions. Local inhabitants, confronted with the tasks of daily survival, cannot be expected to respond to appeals for altruistic self-sacrifice. Consequently, forests are cut and burned for short-term economic gains. This problem is often exacerbated by misguided government policies in many countries, such as government-sponsored timber concessions that promote inefficient harvest levels, tree selection, and reforestation levels. Governments may charge a royalty far below the true economic value of the standing forest. Such low royalties and special tax breaks raise the profits of logging companies, which thereby stimulate timber booms. In addition, some governments provide special land tenure rules or tax benefits to individuals who "improve" the land by clearing the forest. These rules encourage development in the rain forest region because they impel poor settlers to seek land for agriculture and wealthy landowners to look for new investments.

Commercial and Industrial Products
Derived from Tropical Rain Forests

Product	Value of imports by region (millions of U.S. dollars)	Market share of rain forest products (percent)	Region receiving imports	Year of estimate
Commercial Products				
Fruit and vegetable juices	4,000	100	World	1988
Cut flowers	2,500	100	World	1985
Food additives	750	100	United States, European Community	1991
Spices	439	small	United States	1987
Nuts	216	100	World	1988
Food colorings	140	10	World	1987
Vitamins	67	small	United States	1990
Fiber	54	100	United States	1983/4
Industrial Products				
Fuel	60,000	<1	United States	1984
Pesticides	16,000	1	World	1987
Natural rubber	666	100	United States	1978
Tannins	170	large	United States	1980
Construction material	12	1	United States	1984
Natural waxes	9.3	100	United States	1985

Note: James Duke, an economic botanist at the U.S. Department of Agriculture, has been compiling estimates of the economic value of hundreds of key commercial and industrial rain forest products. Some of the important estimates are summarized here. Although not all of the imported products are derived from tropical rain forest countries, Duke claims that they all have the potential to be sustainably harvested from these regions.

Source: James Duke, "Tropical Botanical Extractives" (Unpublished manuscript, U.S. Department of Agriculture, Washington, D.C., April 1989).

Environmental entrepreneurs can create commercial alternatives to the traditional damaging uses of rain forest resources, but several factors must first be taken into consideration. For example, commercial development cannot be allowed to harm the ecological integrity of the ecosystem. This can be a difficult challenge as the scale of production increases for many projects. Also, if existing firms are profitable, new firms will be attracted into the industry, thus placing additional pressure on the fragile ecosystem. Of course, the product must also pass the test of the market; consumers must be willing to pay a price that covers the full cost of production. Some environmentally conscious consumers may be willing to pay a premium for sustainably harvested rain forest products. The size of this "green premium" would depend upon these consumers' willingness and ability to pay, as well as on the prices of other products competing with the rain forest products. To maintain the green premium over time, environmental entrepreneurs need to devise a strategy that differentiates their products from others through advertising and some type of institutionalized labeling system. These entrepreneurs must also anticipate the effect of expanding output on market prices. Previous studies have examined the market value of sustainable products from a single hectare. One study in the Amazonian rain forest in Peru found that sustainably harvested products such as fruit, nuts, rubber latex, and selectively logged timber yield more net value than do plantation forestry and cattle ranching. If harvests are expanded, however, market prices may be pushed down, and the profitability of the program reduced. Another consideration is that entrepreneurs may be able to avoid the expense of developing extensive distribution networks and other marketing costs by forming alliances with established commercial firms. These firms typically have retail outlets and experienced business personnel that can assist the small entrepreneur.

Finally, the environmental entrepreneur must channel income back to the effective owners of the rain forests—the local indigenous people. This return raises the issue of rain forest property rights. The property rights over rain forest resources are not well defined or enforced. Rain forest land is often held collectively, and government-owned land marked as a reserve is not always protected. Even private landowners have a difficult time preventing landless squatters from using their property. Without the enforcement of property rights, rain forests become an open-access resource that is overexploited. This result is not inevitable, however. History suggests that, when the benefits of establishing new property rights exceed the costs, societies often devise new ways to define property rights and improve the allocation of resources.

Intellectual Property Rights

In addition to the question of physical property rights, there is the problem of defining intellectual property rights. Indigenous people possess a wealth of esoteric knowledge about local plants and animals and their usages. Conservation groups argue that the wisdom of the local inhabitants must be given an economic value or else that knowledge will disappear amidst the destruction of the forest. At the same time, scientists and entrepreneurs also contribute value to rain forest products by discovering useful medicinal compounds in the plants. If these interests are not protected, there will not be sufficient economic incentive to develop new products. During the Earth Summit in Rio de Janeiro in the summer of 1992, the Bush administration refused to sign an international treaty on biodiversity on the grounds that it would harm the interests of biotechnology firms. (The Clinton administration signed the biodiversity treaty on 4 June 1993.) A key challenge is to develop an institutional mechanism that recognizes the value of both the natives' knowledge and the scientists' and entrepreneurs' contributions, and therefore rewards both types of intellectual property rights in the development of rain forest products.

The Tagua Initiative

Conservation International is an environmental organization based in Washington, D.C., that works to conserve biodiversity by supporting local rain forest communities world-wide. Through a project entitled "The Tagua Initiative," Conservation International is attempting to synthesize "the approaches of business, community development, and applied science to promote conservation through the marketing of nontimber forest products." The tagua nut is an ivory-like seed that is harvested from tropical palm trees to make buttons, jewelry, chess pieces, carvings, and other arts and crafts. Conservation International links button manufacturers in the United States and other countries with rural tagua harvesters in the endangered rain forests of Esmeraldas in Ecuador. The organization works independently with participating companies to design unique marketing strategies tailored to those companies' individual images, product offerings, and marketing campaigns.

In 1990, Conservation International began expanding the market for tagua products and developing a local industry around tagua. Today, tagua buttons are being used by 24 clothing companies, including such major manufacturers as Smith & Hawken, Esprit, J. Crew, and L.L. Bean. The current distribution network links the Ecuadorian tagua producers to the clothing companies through four wholesale button manufacturers. Conservation International collects a royalty based on a percentage of sales to wholesale button manufacturers and uses the proceeds to support local conservation and community development programs in the rain forest. It has also focused its efforts on developing a viable local tagua industry that includes harvesting and manufacturing. A primary objective of the Tagua Initiative is to provide the 1,200 local harvesters with an attractive price for tagua so that they have an economic incentive to protect the standing forest. Recent figures indicate that the price paid to tagua collectors has risen 92 percent since the program began (a 32 percent real price increase after adjusting for the estimated inflation rate). To increase the flow of income to the native economy, Conservation International encourages the development of new tagua products that can be manufactured locally. Currently, the tagua production line has expanded to include eight manufacturers of jewelry, arts and crafts, and other items.

The Tagua Initiative provides a tremendously successful example, at least in the initial stages of development. Since February 1990, 850 tons of tagua have been delivered directly to factories, and the program has generated approximately $2 million in button sales to manufacturers in North America, Europe, and Japan. According to Robin Frank, tagua product manager at Conservation International, the organization is collaborating with about 50 companies worldwide, and many others have expressed interest. Moreover, the Tagua Initiative in Ecuador has become a role model for new projects in Colombia, Guatemala, Peru, the Philippines, and a number of other countries. In all of these cases, Conservation International is working with local organizations to identify and develop sustainable commercial products in a manner that protects sensitive ecosystems. These projects are expanding the rain forest product line to Brazil nuts and pecans from Peru, fibers for textiles, and waxes and oils for the personal health and hygiene market.

Local Conservation

In addition to creating marketable rain forest products, Conservation International cooperates with conservation and community development programs, such as the Corporacion de Investigaciones para el Desarrollo Socio/Ambiental (CIDESA) in Ecuador. Ecologists, economic botanists, and conservation planners affiliated with Conservation International help CIDESA to identify critical rain forest sites and monitor harvesting practices to ensure their sustainability, among other things. The province of Esmeraldas in Ecuador is considered a critical "hot spot" because it contains some of the highest levels of biodiversity in Latin America and harbors some of Ecuador's last remaining pristine tracts of western Andean rain forest. Coincidentally, it is one of Ecuador's poorest communities, with a meager annual average per-capita income of $600, about one-half of the national average. The community of Comuna Rio Santiago in Esmeraldas has a population of 70,000, which grows dramatically at an annual rate of 3.7 percent. Four out of every 10 children suffer from malnutrition, and the infant mortality rate is 60 per 1,000 births. There is a high level of alcoholism, and drug addiction is a growing problem. Life expectancy is just 50 years, and the illiteracy level is near 50 percent. All of these actualities indicate an urgent need to protect the natural resources found in this region, not only to maintain biodiversity but also to ensure the economic welfare of the local inhabitants. If these needs are addressed, the program will have the potential to change the current low standard of living in Ecuador by promoting both conservation and economic development.

Over the next 10 years, Conservation International plans to increase the use of numerous rain forest products, such as medicines, furniture, and baskets. These efforts can serve as a role model for firms in the industrialized world that seek to create rain forest products and improve the well-being of rain forest inhabitants. . . .

A Key to Preservation

Clearly, sustainable development of rain forest products has the potential to bring about positive change, preserve biodiversity, and improve the welfare of local communities. Because deforestation is spiraling out of control, the efforts of organizations like Conservation International . . . have become imperative.

"The drug industry, in its search for breakthroughs in medication, has come to see that the conservation of . . . tropical rainforests is very much in its own interest."

Pharmaceutical Discoveries Can Help Preserve the Rain Forests

Sam Thernstrom

Sam Thernstrom is a research fellow at the Political Economy Research Center, an environmental think tank in Bozeman, Montana. In the following viewpoint, Thernstrom maintains that drug companies are now searching for new cures for medical problems in the plant life of the rain forests. Thernstrom contends that the medicines drug companies develop from rain forest products may provide the profit levels necessary to convince local residents that protecting the rain forest from further destruction is ultimately more lucrative than logging them or clearing the trees for growing crops. These drugs, he asserts, may be the key to ending the devastation of tropical forests.

As you read, consider the following questions:

1. How many plant and animal species are estimated to be in the rain forests, according to Thernstrom?
2. How does the relationship between Merck and INBio function, according to the author?

Sam Thernstrom, "Jungle Fever," *New Republic*, April 19, 1993. Reprinted by permission of the *New Republic*, ©1993, The New Republic, Inc.

Environmentalists should be quietly, cautiously celebrating pharmaceutical companies. The drug industry, in its search for breakthroughs in medication, has come to see that conservation of natural resources, and especially of tropical rainforests, is very much in its own interest. The notion that mysterious tropical plants and animals might yield new cures may have at one time seemed farfetched. But recent work in tropical biology has established that the vast majority of species on Earth await discovery. Scientists have identified some 1.4 million species of organisms so far. Only since the 1980s, as tropical deforestation rates have soared, have biologists begun to see what they're missing. Some estimate that there are as many as 50 million species. And while that figure may be high, even conservative estimates place the minimum number at 5 million, and an upper range of 30 million is not implausible.

Forests and Species Are Destroyed

These facts alone may not impress: Why should anyone care about the millions of unknown insects crawling about unknown trees in tropical forests? We find it hard to appreciate a resource that cannot be cut down, dug up, pumped out or eaten, and even harder to speculate on the value of unknown flowers and beetles. "Biodiversity," says Harvard biologist E.O. Wilson, "is our most valuable but least appreciated resource." He could have added "least developed." For as the forests are destroyed, these millions of unknown species are likely being destroyed along with them.

Setting aside, for the moment, the myriad moral and ethical questions that such mass destruction raises, there are also practical concerns: in destroying undiscovered species, we lose unique information. There's no way to know just how useful that information could be. But it is virtually certain that out of the many millions of species, there are bound to be at least a few plants that will never be discovered.

Jalisco maize almost met with this fate. When this species of corn was discovered in Mexico by a graduate student in the 1970s, its entire population was confined to just twenty-five acres of mountainside. And this would have been destroyed within a week, since the land was slated to be cleared for farming. Jalisco maize has the potential to become a multibillion-dollar crop: it is resistant to many diseases and, unlike other existing corn species, it is a perennial.

Medicinal Value

And while the agricultural potential of yet unknown species is surely significant, the greatest practical value of our unknown biodiversity may be medicinal. In the United States one-quarter of all prescriptions are filled with drugs made from plant extracts; aspirin is derived from an unheralded plant, meadowsweet. Another 13 percent of our drugs are derived from microorganisms, and 3 percent from animals; in all, 41 percent of our medicines are derived from living things.

Saving the Forests

A few visionary pharmaceutical companies are once again looking to the rain forest for drugs that could yield a windfall. But this time around, the customary practice of "ripping off the natives" is strictly verboten. These enlightened firms insist that cultures whose tribal lore leads to important discoveries be compensated with money, goods, or services.

Why pay for what can be gotten for free? To protect endangered people and plants and—always the bottom line in business—to ensure future profits.

With a juggernaut of ranchers and farmers flattening 115,000 acres of pristine rain forest a day and the indigenous Indians vanishing even faster than the trees, the new brand of conservation-minded business people believe their scheme will provide an economically viable means of preserving the world's richest ecosystem and the people such as the Makushi Indians who know how to manage it wisely.

Omni, July 1993.

Despite the success drug companies have had with plant-based drugs, in the last several decades pharmaceutical research has focused heavily on man-made compounds. Analyzing plants is time consuming and expensive, and most plants turn out to be useless as medicine. As a result, fewer than 3 percent of the world's known flowering plants have even been screened for medicinally useful compounds. But recently the focus has begun to shift back to the biological world. As Charles McChesney of the University of Mississippi explains, "The synthetic chemists have made the easy molecules"; new plants now seem worth investigating. It's also easier to do so since recent technological advancements have made it possible to screen huge numbers of compounds quickly.

Recent discoveries of plants with lucrative medicinal value have helped to rekindle the interest of the drug industry. One of the greatest modern advances in cancer treatment, for example, was nothing more than a remarkable accident: while examining the rosy periwinkle of Madagascar for anti-diuretic qualities during the mid-1980s, chemists found two powerful alkaloids, vinblastine and vincristine, which proved to be the most effective cures we know for two particularly deadly cancers, Hodgkin's disease and acute lymphocytic leukemia. Survival rates are up from 2 percent to 58 percent and from 20 percent to 80 percent respectively, and sales of these two drugs now total $180 million a year.

The Forests' Value

Both pharmaceutical companies and conservationists took note of the rosy periwinkle. Conservationists were delighted at the discovery, since it offered dramatic proof of a popular theme: biodiversity is worth saving. But that didn't mean it was going to be saved: none of the profits from the periwinkle went to conserving the forests in which it was found. This was particularly distressing since that same habitat may well have contained other plants or insects of equal or greater value. Conservation biologists realized they could not afford to repeat that mistake. The result was a ground-breaking partnership between Merck & Co., the largest pharmaceutical company in the United States, and Costa Rica's National Institute for Biodiversity, INBio. Their agreement, signed in September 1991, is widely regarded as the next great hope for financing conservation in the tropics. A *New York Times* editorial in 1992 hailed the Merck-INBio partnership as one that "shows the way" for progress on biotechnology issues, issues that the United States had been unable to resolve with other countries at the Earth Summit.

Under the terms of the agreement, Merck provides INBio with $1 million, plus $180,000 worth of research equipment, which INBio has used to support a team of thirty-one "parataxonomists" who comb Costa Rica's forests searching for new plant and animal species. The team members are native Costa Ricans, trained in species identification and collection. And they've been remarkably successful. Each parataxonomist brings in up to 5,000 insects and fifty plant specimens each month. Costa Rica may harbor 500,000 species, many of which are only found in very limited habitats. Arthropods (insects, spiders) alone may account for 300,000 species, of which only one-fifth have been described.

In return for its support, INBio gives Merck plant and insect samples, which it screens for valuable compounds. From a pharmaceutical point of view, the beauty of the tropics is not only that they contain a phenomenal number of species, but that the species density is so high and the evolutionary struggle so richly developed that many of the plants and insects have evolved sophisticated chemical defenses. These defenses—which are often very potent—are also often medically valuable. Alkaloids such as morphine and nicotine are commonly found in the tropics, as are other medicinally useful compounds such as phenolics, tannins (found in cecropias and mangroves, both of which are abundant in the tropics), cyanogenic glycosides (found in passionflowers and manioca) and terpenoids, which are found in more than thirty species of Costa Rican dry forest plants. So the potential for success is high.

The Merck-INBio partnership is more than just another example of industry realizing there's money to be made in conservation. It represents a growing trend in conservation biology toward placing conservation in a larger social context. Should Merck successfully market new drugs derived from the INBio plant samples, a large portion of the profits will return to protect the habitat.

It's this last step that, naturally, conservationists are most enthusiastic about. Yet it may also prove to be the most problematic. "Chemical prospecting" is a slow and expensive process, as is bringing a new drug to market. And though tropical deforestation rates have dropped significantly in some countries, overall they remain very high. Unless something is done to stop it, the researchers may be too late.

"A rain forest left standing is worth more than the wood or the next best use if the forest were cut down."

Ecotourism Can Help Preserve the Rain Forests

Peter Davison

Ecotourism brings travelers to remote and environmentally sensitive locations needing preservation in order to foster interest in those locations. In the following viewpoint, Peter Davison, poetry editor for the *Atlantic Monthly*, recounts his journey to a remote hotel in the Amazon rain forest. He presents the rain forest he visited as an unspoiled, beautiful area that has been protected from destruction because the hotel's owners have resisted further development of the area. Davison suggests that ecotourism contributed to this rain forest's conservation.

As you read, consider the following questions:

1. What were the goals of the hotel's owners when they purchased their property, according to the author?
2. According to Davison, why do the hotel's owners resist expanding their operation?

Excerpted from Peter Davison, "Between the Sea and the Jungle," *Atlantic Monthly*, July 1995. Reprinted by permission.

Augusto Rodríguez is a supple, talkative, graying man who walks with unaffected grace; he wears rubber boots and a small hat and carries a long stick as he leads us under the canopy of the rain forest, on the Pacific coast of Costa Rica. We four gringos, guests at the Lapa Rios resort, follow him along a narrow trail that winds through the gloom down a hill toward a stream hustling noisily in our near future. Augusto comes to a stop and seems to sniff the air. "There is an animal nearby," he announces in his strongly accented English. He inches across the slope, wary and alert, and points to something we cannot see. "Curasao," I think he says, and then he begins shuffling forward, stooped and chanting as he creeps toward the "animal," which we are soon able to make out as a dingy bird, roughly the size and shape of a guinea fowl, standing motionless on the ground beneath a massive strangler fig tree.

Augusto chants as though he were a priest, in a singsong that might be part of a black mass in an abandoned chapel. The "curasao," which *Birds of Costa Rica* will later identify as a "*gallina de monte*" (*Tinamus major*), has been entirely disarmed. We approach, and it doesn't stir. Augusto has hypnotized it. Immobile, it stares at its watchers without affect, a remote and ineffectual bird. How long will it stay like this? Half an hour, Augusto says firmly, and he leads us onward.

We descend to a waterfall we have been hearing in the background, and climb past it up another slope. "White-winged dove," Augusto says solemnly, handing us a feather he has picked up from the ground; he moves on, and then stops and points to a "quinine tree." A little later he points out another tree, which "produces milk you use to keep from getting acid in the stomach." Next he hands us some berries, asking us to smell them. "Citronella lemon. It opens the breathing tubes, opens the valves of the heart."

Augusto has already told us that his father was English and his mother was Indian, and that he is a shaman. We fork off the narrow trail, and he stops, as he has done at each junction, to place his hands together and, with bowed head, murmur a prayer for safety on the next leg. Furry gray fragments fall from the balsa trees above. Another tree has spines growing up its trunk. Augusto points out a procession of leaf-cutting ants crossing our path, and a black spider in a huge web. A sudden crash, and a crested eagle flaps hugely away under the trees, to disappear at length into the forest canopy. . . .

Moving to the Rain Forest

It is before breakfast. I am talking with John Lewis under the canopy at the entrance to Lapa Rios. Lewis, a spare, trim, bristly man with a capacity for crisp utterance, says, "We came here and fell in love with the people, the country, the geography, the climate. A country without violence, no standing army, democracy. I was sitting on the balcony of the hotel at Quepos after about five beers, and I suddenly thought, How about if we do a resort for birders in Costa Rica?" John and Karen Lewis were in the Peace Corps in Africa in the 1960s. John for twenty years conducted a very successful law practice in Minneapolis, and Karen taught music, but neither of them ever forgot those far-off years. "Though we didn't know it at the time, they were the best two years of our lives," John says. When they took their young children back to Kenya in 1988, the whole memory of their dedicated youth came back. Then John's father died. The result was a reappraisal.

Ecotourism and Economics

If ecotourism is successfully introduced into an area threatened by, for example, logging or overfishing, ecotourism can give local residents a reason to leave the trees standing or the reef intact as they get jobs as guides or hoteliers. What becomes apparent to anyone who visits a developing country is that economic survival is a pressing and persistent concern. A conservationist working in Costa Rica once put it, "If we want the forest to be maintained, the bottom line is we have to produce cold, hard cash for the campesino."

Lisa Jones, *Buzzworm*, March/April 1993.

They decided to quit their jobs and settle in a tropical climate, near the sea, and engage in something involved with tourism. They polled travel agents and were told that they would do best to establish an inn in the wilderness that could offer high-quality accommodations and service. Where? In 1990 they narrowed the search to Costa Rica's Pacific coast, and made six trips there. John wandered down to the Osa Peninsula, which boasted only one road and whose principal town, Puerto Jiménez, had once been a Panamanian prison camp. At the far end of the road John found himself overlooking the Pacific Ocean from a hilltop clearing where there was land for sale: a thousand acres, with five rivers, forty waterfalls, and a view to eternity—a perfect place for a small hotel. "This is the place," he radioed Karen, "but it's four times our budget." "Buy it," she replied. "We'll figure out how to pay for it." They cashed in everything: their house, his law practice, their retirement fund, and their savings. A Minneapolis architect helped the Lewises design a simple and beautiful system of thatched buildings, each with a magnificent exposure to views, air, ocean, and forest. By early 1993 Lapa Rios ("Rivers of the Scarlet Macaw") had been designed and built and was in operation, with Karen as building superintendent, interior designer, and ambiance controller, and John as financial manager, personnel manager, marketing director, and supervisor of supply, transportation, and legal services.

Lapa Rios is no ordinary hotel. It can serve about thirty guests at a time and has a staff of thirty-three. In less than three years it has made a reputation for itself among aficionados of ecotourism. But John and Karen Lewis have goals other than merely running a successful luxury hotel: to raise capital for the acquisition and preservation of endangered land; to disseminate information about deforestation, reforestation, and rain-forest preservation; and to work with the local community to help demonstrate that a rain forest left standing is worth more than the wood or the next best use if the forest were cut down.

The Ecotourist Experience

We arrive in Puerto Jiménez, approaching in a thirty-passenger plane across the waters of Golfo Dulce to touch down at a dirt airstrip next to a cemetery, a faintly sinister spot reminiscent of the opening pages of Graham Greene's *The Power and the Glory.* John Lewis is there to deliver a few departing guests to the same loop flight that has brought us from San Jose, the capital, in a little over an hour. Once they have boarded the plane, he escorts us and our bags to an open truck. We bounce happily on wooden seats in the back for about forty-five minutes along a dirt road that leads between pastures where Brahma cattle lie in the shade of large trees, and across several shallow fords whose waters gurgle around our wheels. Cattle egrets stand everywhere, on the backs of the cattle, on the ground at their sides. The roadside is splashed with bright heliconia blossoms of red and yellow, with the scarlet blooms of wild ginger and banana trees.

The truck stops to shift into four-wheel drive, and a large bird with a long, dark, thick neck that in this late-morning light looks yellow in the front flaps a few strokes and lands by a stream, examining us out of one orange eye; it is a bare-throated tiger-heron (*Tigrisoma mexicanum*). The air is quite hot and getting hotter, and we are glad when the truck starts up again and the breeze can cool our sweat. The woods are growing deeper, but most of the land on both sides is fenced off by posts formed by slender living trees. Now and then we see a thatched or tin-roofed building—a house? a school? A fenced-in plantation of trees carries a sign that says STON FORESTAL. (This refers to the Stone Container Corporation, one of the world's largest manufacturers of corrugated paper products. Those trees are being grown on land rented from local farmers. It will take just under twenty years to grow three crops of pulpwood here. After Stone's lease expires, the owners may use the spent land as they will.)

After a particularly splashy ford, we zag to the left up a steep slope, and then zig to the right, still more steeply, while a vast expanse of Pacific Ocean opens up below us. We pass through an entrance gate and whine still *more* steeply to a level parking place beyond which rises, perhaps fifty feet into the air, a peaked thatched roof. Smiling, Karen Lewis comes forward to welcome us to Lapa Rios. A young man, in halting English, begins to offer us a drink, but he is interrupted by a thunderous huffing-groaning sound: uh uh *uh* UH UH *UH*. "Can you hear the howler monkeys?" Karen asks, enthusiastically but unnecessarily, for they seem to be at our shoulder. The young man now brings my wife and me tall, cool glasses of fruit punch, each adorned with a butter-yellow blossom. Under the high straw roof containing a lookout above our heads we walk forward, sipping, to a breathtaking verandah lookout, which faces south on the open Pacific, southeast on Golfo Dulce. To the southwest and west a 270-degree view of the coastal rain forest spreads out and up. There is not a boat to be seen on the water, but overhead wheel white hawks and black vultures. The hot sky is brilliantly blue. Soon we are escorted to our bungalow, down 146 steps. On a dazzling white wall a gecko lizard is perched upside down next to the doorknob that opens a locked door into a high thatched room, deeply shaded now at midmorning, with its own terrace, indoor-and-outdoor shower, closets and tables, chairs and overhead fan, two huge firm beds, mosquito netting, and screen walls with bamboo blinds to keep out the heat of the day. We look at each other and sigh. Eternal honeymooners.

When we climb back up the steps past the swimming pool for lunch (gazpacho, a tomato stuffed with tuna, tropical fruit), we are further persuaded that we have gone to heaven. Dinner by candlelight (fish ceviche, fresh grilled tuna, fresh vegetables, flan, white Chilean wine), with Glenn Gould's Bach Partitas in the background, confirms that belief. The moon rises full over the Pacific. As we descend to our bungalow, the huge red eyes of common pauraques, or nighthawks, stare at our approach and then flit away. We fall asleep under our mosquito nets (though there are no mosquitos) to the mewing of tiny birds, the rustle of palm leaves, the occasional cry of nocturnal animals hunting one another in the rain forest.

The Dream

Karen Lewis says, "Someone told us about a movie that came out when we were down here, called *Field of Dreams:* 'If you build it, they will come.' So we came and we did what we said we would do, and surprised the community in the Osa, because they kept waiting for a two-hundred-room hotel to be built here. We came here to be a model of how to do something. Tourism has grown too quickly in Costa Rica for the quality of service to grow. 'Good' is not enough."

Lapa Rios has been built, and they have come: The traffic in the dry season (December to April) is all that the Lewises can handle, but they have no intention of expanding. "That's no solution," Karen says. John and Karen were both hoping for a higher achievement. Karen says, "There is something almost spiritual here—looking at the ocean; feeling the breeze out of the rain forest; listening to the howler monkeys, the insects that are always humming, the cicadas and crickets and whatnot; watching the moon come up and just spill its light." John says, "This isn't only a piece of land; it's an organism. . . . When we bought it, we thought it was beautiful, but now people have come from everywhere, and we know it's a very special forest."

Eighty-five percent of the guests at Lapa Rios are from the United States. The rest are for the most part German, Swiss, and Canadian. The tourists who come must, of course, be fairly affluent, though the rates are not unreasonable: $120 per day per person, all meals and local transport included, with drinks and tours extra. Guests ought to be hale and hearty to enjoy the occasional rigors of outdoor rain-forest life. Children under five are not encouraged to come, because metropolitan safety standards cannot apply to an inn built on a hilltop with precipitous slopes falling away to a rain forest inhabited by boa constrictors and tarantulas.

The Green Season

The Lewises wish—and not only for economic reasons—that more tourists would come in what Karen calls the "green season": May to November. John says, "It's cooler. It's greener. It's the mud season. It's quieter. The people who live here like it better than the dry season. It rains in the afternoons and the evenings primarily. Our guests are as happy here in the rainy season as in the dry. We do the tours: it's more exciting. A couple of times we've had to hire a farm tractor to get them to their flights. You can't believe the intensity of rain."

The Lewises have other wishes as well. Karen says, "Our prime focus coming here was to preserve the forest—our first reason. Now we're being pushed by our staff: 'Why don't you build me a house for my family? Let me bring my wife, and I'll stay.' There is all this pressure on us to build a company town, but we came here to preserve the forest."

They had hoped to create a model for ecotourism. And what is ecotourism? That's not quite clear as yet—not in practice. Does the emphasis fall on ecology or on economics? The Lewises have certainly felt the conflict. "Four years ago," John says, "there was very little traffic on the road—a vehicle once every two days. Now everyone wants to be in the wilderness but wants to be near someplace that is established, near the 'private nature reserve.' Since the building of Lapa Rios, land values on the Osa Peninsula have gone up between five hundred and a thousand percent." John, with deep regret, expects to see a lot of building by people who say they are conservationists but who will in practice be chipping away at the rain forest.

As John makes this doleful prediction, sitting in the shaded entrance to Lapa Rios at 7:00 A.M., he suddenly freezes. *"A white hawk just came and landed in the trees not more than forty feet away!"* My tape records a *skrawk* of birdcall, a skitter of feet, hushed exclamations in the background. The hawk (*Leucopternis albicollis*) crouches on a low branch, at eye level, blinking, weaving, and glaring at us, Marine to Marine. Who owns this forest anyhow?

Preserving the Wilderness

The hawk flies away. John goes on: "My idea was that we could be an outpost in the wilderness for years and years, and that things around us would stay pretty much the same. People would enjoy our wilderness and our food and our accommodations and go back. Being a model demonstration unit means that we have motivated a lot of people to come and move next to us and eliminate the buffer of wilderness right next to our preserve. On the other hand, there are people who have bought fifteen hundred acres right next to us, and they *are* going to preserve those pieces. They are doing that on the assurance that *we* will be here. In terms of acreage we have probably accounted for a large increase in the preservation of forest that had been slated for potential destruction.

"We thought we were going to motivate conservationists; but the real outcome is that we *have* motivated visitors to take a serious look at their lives. Yes, the forest needs to be dedicated. It's a private nature reserve because we say it is." That bold statement raises nagging questions that make a tourist uneasy as he watches for toucans and howler monkeys in the green forest canopy outside Lapa Rios. The sea and the jungle belong to no one, not to the awed visitor, not to the innkeeper, not to the dedicated shaman, not even to the "Rich Coast" of Central America.

Periodical Bibliography

The following articles have been selected to supplement the diverse views presented in this chapter. Addresses are provided for periodicals not indexed in the *Readers' Guide to Periodical Literature*, the *Alternative Press Index*, or the *Social Sciences Index*.

Rob Buchanan
"Looking for Rainforest Heroes," *Utne Reader*, March/April 1993.

Stephen Corry
"Harvest Hype," *Our Planet*, vol. 6, no. 4, 1994. Available from PO Box 30552, Nairobi, Kenya.

Polly Ghazi
"The Continuing Fight for the Amazon," *World Press Review*, September 1994.

Malcolm Gillis
"Tropical Deforestation: Poverty, Population, and Public Policy," *Vital Speeches of the Day*, April 1, 1996.

Diane Jukofsky
"Can Marketing Save the Rainforest?" *E Magazine*, July/August 1993.

Mac Margolis
"Taking Two Steps Back," *Newsweek*, January 8, 1996.

Susan Meeker-Lowry
"Killing Them Softly: The 'Rainforest Harvest,'" *Z Magazine*, July/August 1993.

Susan Meeker-Lowry
"Who Is Destroying the Rainforests?" *Z Magazine*, May 1993.

Erin B. Newman
"Earth's Vanishing Medicine Cabinet: Rain Forest Destruction and Its Impact on the Pharmaceutical Industry," *American Journal of Law & Medicine*, vol. 20, no. 4, 1994. Available from 765 Commonwealth Ave., Suite 1634, Boston, MA 02215.

Mark Richardson
"Wrestling with the Preservation of the Korup Rain Forest," *Our Planet*, vol. 5, no. 4, 1993.

Philip Shenon
"Hunt in Forests of Borneo Aims to Track Down Natural Drugs," *New York Times*, December 6, 1994.

David Tenenbaum
"Drawing a Green Line: Costa Rica Makes Audacious Plans to Reclaim Its Forests," *E Magazine*, March/April 1995.

USA Today
"Saving Rainforests May Be Doomed," April 1994.

Harry J. Van Buren
"Why Business Should Help Save the Rainforests," *Business and Society Review*, Fall 1995. Available from 25-13 Old Kings Highway N., Suite 107, Darien, CT 06820.

World Press Review
"Colombia's Vanishing Forests," June 1993.

For Further Discussion

Chapter 1

1. Robert T. Watson concedes that there is no definitive proof of human-induced global warming, but he insists that evidence "points in that direction." What evidence does he present? What evidence does Jeffrey Salmon give to dispute the theory of human-caused global warming? Whose use of evidence is more convincing? Explain your answer using examples from the viewpoints.

2. Robert Jastrow is the president of the George C. Marshall Institute, a research organization that has consistently questioned the validity of global warming science and the seriousness of global warming as an environmental threat. Does this information about Jastrow's professional background influence your evaluation of his arguments? If so, in what way?

3. Ross Gelbspan writes that S. Fred Singer has received consulting fees from various oil companies. Does this statement affect your evaluation of Singer's viewpoint? If so, how? Does it influence your reading of Gelbspan's viewpoint? Explain.

4. Based on the viewpoints in this chapter, do you agree with Gelbspan's assertion that the oil and coal industries are engaged in a public relations campaign to downplay the threat of global warming? Why or why not?

Chapter 2

1. William K. Stevens reports on a scientific study that blames human activities for global warming. Frederick Seitz maintains that nature plays a much larger role in global warming than human activity does. On what aspects of global warming do Seitz and the study discussed by Stevens agree? How do they disagree? Does Stevens's review of the study successfully counter Seitz's argument? Why or why not?

2. In their viewpoints, Nigel Calder and Richard A. Kerr both discuss the scientific study of Danish researchers Eigil Friis-Christensen and Knud Lassen, but they come to opposite conclusions. In your opinion, whose conclusion is more valid? Support your answer with examples from the viewpoints.

Chapter 3

1. George J. Mitchell argues that the devastation of unchecked global warming—floods, droughts, and the extinction of plants and animals—will equal that of nuclear war. Thomas Gale Moore disagrees with Mitchell's argument and asserts that global warming would affect the Earth in many beneficial ways. Which scenario do you think is more likely to occur? Why?

2. David E. Pitt reports on a study that predicts famine in developing countries if greenhouse gas emissions are not curtailed. John Reilly maintains that it is unlikely that global warming will produce famine if poverty is eliminated in these Third World countries. Which viewpoint do you find more convincing? Explain.

Chapter 4

1. Christopher Flavin and Odil Tunali contend that the burning of fossil fuels (such as coal and oil) is largely responsible for the global warming crisis. They blame the lobbying efforts of the American Petroleum Institute, among others, for promoting political opposition to measures designed to reduce fossil fuel emissions. William F. O'Keefe argues that not enough is known about global warming to justify the unreasonable expense of reducing carbon emissions. Does the fact that O'Keefe is the executive vice president of the American Petroleum Institute influence your assessment of his viewpoint? Explain your answer.

2. In his viewpoint, Al Gore maintains that global warming is a serious threat to the planet and that efforts to fight global warming must be taken immediately to avert worldwide disaster. Robert C. Balling Jr. contends that steps to combat global warming can be safely delayed until more is known about the phenomenon. With which viewpoint do you agree more? Why?

Chapter 5

1. Anjali Acharya argues that the international community should protect rain forests through treaties and initiatives. Evaluate the effectiveness of her solution. What are the likely drawbacks and benefits? Mark Clayton contends that political pressure from environmentalists and local groups on countries that purchase wood from rain forests can help to save these forests. Compare the effectiveness of his solution with Acharya's. Are there any similarities in their arguments? Explain your answer.

2. Examine the solution to rain forest destruction offered by Thomas A. Carr, Heather L. Pedersen, and Sunder Ramaswamy. How do sustainable development projects work? Do you consider this solution effective? Why or why not? Compare this viewpoint with Sam Thernstrom's. Are their solutions similar? Explain your answer with examples from the viewpoints.

3. Ecotourism has been used in Costa Rica and other Latin American countries to preserve sensitive rain forests. What preservation benefits of ecotourism does Peter Davison relate in his viewpoint? Does he discuss any potential problems in using ecotourism to preserve the rain forest? If so, what are they? In your opinion, do the potential benefits of ecotourism outweigh the possible problems? Explain.

Organizations to Contact

The editors have compiled the following list of organizations concerned with the issues debated in this book. The descriptions are derived from materials provided by the organizations. All have publications or information available for interested readers. The list was compiled on the date of publication of the present volume; names, addresses, phone and fax numbers, and e-mail addresses may change. Be aware that many organizations take several weeks or longer to respond to inquiries, so allow as much time as possible.

The Atmosphere Alliance
PO Box 10346
Olympia, WA 98502
(360) 352-1763
fax: (360) 943-4977

The alliance works to restabilize the chemical balance in the earth's atmosphere that shapes world climate and shields life from deadly ultraviolet radiation. It seeks to inform and support citizens who try to implement public policies that will substantially reduce atmospheric pollution. The alliance publishes the quarterly newsletter *No Sweat News* and the citizen action guide *Life Support!*

Competitive Enterprise Institute (CEI)
1001 Connecticut Ave. NW, Suite 1250
Washington, DC 20036
(202) 331-1010
fax: (202) 331-0640
e-mail: info@cei.org
web site: http://www.cei.org

CEI encourages the use of private incentives and property rights to protect the environment. It advocates removing governmental barriers in order to establish a system in which the private sector would be responsible for the environment. CEI's publications include the monthly newsletter *CEI Update*, the book *The True State of the Planet*, and the monograph *Federal Agriculture Policy: A Harvest of Environmental Abuse*.

The George C. Marshall Institute
1730 M St. NW, Suite 502
Washington, DC 20036
(202) 296-9655
fax: (202) 296-9714
e-mail: 71553.3017@compuserve.com

The institute is a research group that provides scientific and technical advice and promotes scientific literacy on matters that have an impact on public policy. It is dedicated to providing policy makers and the public with rigorous, clearly written, and unbiased technical analyses of public policies, including policy on global warming. The institute's publications include *Global Warming Update*, *The Global Warming Experiment*, and *Global Warming and Ozone Hole Controversies: A Challenge to Scientific Judgment*.

Global Warming International Center (GWIC)
PO Box 5275
Woodridge, IL 60517-0275
(708) 910-1551
fax: (708) 910-1561

GWIC is an international body that disseminates information on science and policy concerning global warming. It serves both governmental and nongovernmental organizations as well as industries in more than one hundred countries. The center sponsors unbiased research supporting the understanding of global warming and its mitigation. It publishes the quarterly newsletter *World Resource Review*.

The Heritage Foundation
214 Massachusetts Ave. NE
Washington, DC 20002
(202) 546-4400
fax: (202) 546-8328

The Heritage Foundation is a conservative think tank that supports free enterprise and limited government in environmental matters. Its publications, such as the quarterly *Policy Review* and the *Heritage Lectures*, include studies on the uncertainty of global warming and the greenhouse effect.

International Society of Tropical Foresters (ISTF)
5400 Grosvenor Ln.
Bethesda, MD 20814
(301) 897-8720
fax: (301) 897-3690

ISTF is an international organization that strives to develop and promote ecologically sound methods of managing and harvesting the world's tropical forests. The society provides information and technical knowledge about the effects of deforestation on agriculture, forestry, industry, and the environment. ISTF publishes the quarterly newsletter *ISTF News*.

Rainforest Action Network (RAN)
450 Sansome St., Suite 700
San Francisco, CA 94111
(415) 398-4404
fax: (415) 398-2732
e-mail: rainforest@ran.org
web site: http://www.ran.org

RAN works to preserve the world's rain forests through activism addressing the logging and importation of tropical timber, cattle ranching in rain forests, and the rights of indigenous rain forest peoples. It also seeks to educate the public about the environmental effects of tropical hardwood logging. RAN's publications include the monthly bulletin *Action Report* and the semiannual *World Rainforest Report*.

Rainforest Alliance
65 Bleecker St.
New York, NY 10012
(212) 677-1900
fax: (212) 677-2187
web site: http://www.rainforest-alliance.org

The alliance is composed of individuals concerned with the conservation of tropical forests. Its members strive to expand awareness of the role the United States plays in the fate of tropical forests and to develop and promote sound alternatives to tropical deforestation. The alliance publishes the bimonthly newsletter the *Canopy*.

Reason Foundation
3415 S. Sepulveda Blvd., Suite 400
Los Angeles, CA 90034-6064
(310) 391-2245
fax: (310) 391-4395

The Reason Foundation is a national public policy research organization. It specializes in a variety of policy areas, including the environment, education, and privatization. The foundation publishes the monthly magazine *Reason* and the books *Global Warming: The Greenhouse, White House, and Poorhouse Effect; The Case Against Electric Vehicle Mandates in California;* and *Solid Waste Recycling Costs—Issues and Answers*.

Sierra Club
85 Second St.
San Francisco, CA 94105
(415) 977-5500
e-mail: activist.desk@sierraclub.org
web site: http://www.sierraclub.org

The Sierra Club is a grassroots organization that promotes the protection and conservation of natural resources. It publishes the bimonthly magazine *Sierra*, the monthly Sierra Club activist resource the *Planet*, and the pamphlet *21 Ways to Help Stop Global Warming*, in addition to numerous books and fact sheets.

Stockholm Environment Institute (SEI)
11 Arlington St.
Boston, MA 02116-3411
(617) 266-8090
fax: (617) 266-8303
e-mail: www.tellus.com
web site: http://www.channel1.com/users/tellus/seib.html

Headquartered in Sweden, SEI is a research institute that operates through an international network. The institute focuses on a variety of environmental issues, including climate change, energy use, and freshwater resources. SEI publishes *SEI: An International Environment Bulletin* four times a year, the *Energy Report* two to three times a year, and *Environmental Perspectives* three times a year.

Union of Concerned Scientists (UCS)
2 Brattle Square
Cambridge, MA 02238-9105
(617) 547-5552
fax: (617) 864-9405
e-mail: menu@ucsusa.org

UCS works to advance responsible public policy in areas where science and technology play a vital role. Its programs focus on safe and renewable energy technologies, transportation reform, arms control, and sustainable agriculture. UCS publications include the quarterly magazine *Nucleus*, the briefing papers *Motor-Vehicle Fuel Efficiency and Global Warming* and *Global Environmental Problems: A Status Report*, and the book *Cool Energy: The Renewable Solution to Global Warming*.

World Resources Institute (WRI)
1709 New York Ave. NW
Washington, DC 20006
(202) 638-6300
fax: (202) 638-0036

WRI conducts policy research on global resources and environmental conditions. It publishes books, reports, and papers; holds briefings, seminars, and conferences; and provides the print and broadcast media with new perspectives and background materials on environmental issues. The institute publishes the books *The Right Climate for Carbon Taxes: Creating Economic Incentives to Protect the Atmosphere* and *The Greenhouse Trap: What We're Doing to the Atmosphere and How We Can Slow Global Warming*.

Worldwatch Institute
1776 Massachusetts Ave. NW
Washington, DC 20036-1904
(202) 452-1999
fax: (202) 296-7365

Worldwatch is a research organization that analyzes and focuses attention on global problems, including environmental concerns such as global warming and the relationship between trade and the environment. It compiles the annual *State of the World* anthology and publishes the bimonthly magazine *World Watch* and the Worldwatch Paper Series, which includes "Clearing the Air: A Global Agenda" and "The Climate of Hope: New Strategies for Stabilizing the World's Atmosphere."

Bibliography of Books

W. Neil Adger and Katrina Brown
Land Use and the Causes of Global Warming. New York: Wiley, 1994.

Anthony B. Anderson
Alternatives to Deforestation: Steps Toward Sustainable Use of the Amazon Rain Forest. New York: Columbia University Press, 1992.

John A. Baden, ed.
Environmental Gore: A Constructive Response to "Earth in the Balance." San Francisco: Pacific Research Institute for Public Policy, 1994.

Robert C. Balling Jr.
The Heated Debate: Greenhouse Predictions Versus Climate Reality. San Francisco: Pacific Research Institute for Public Policy, 1992.

Melvin A. Benarde
Global Warning . . . Global Warming. New York: Wiley, 1992.

Harold W. Bernard Jr.
Global Warming Unchecked: Signs to Watch For. Bloomington: Indiana University Press, 1993.

Lester R. Brown et al.
State of the World 1996: A Worldwatch Institute Report on Progress Toward a Sustainable Society. New York: Norton, 1996.

Seth Cagin and Philip Dray
Between Earth and Sky: How CFCs Changed Our World and Endangered the Ozone Layer. New York: Pantheon, 1993.

William R. Cline
The Economics of Global Warming. Washington, DC: Institute for International Economics, 1992.

Marcus Colchester and Larry Lohmann, eds.
The Struggle for Land and the Fate of the Forests. Atlantic Highlands, NJ: Zed Books, World Rainforest Movement, and *Ecologist,* 1993.

Committee on Science, Engineering, and Public Policy
Policy Implications of Greenhouse Warming. Washington, DC: National Academy Press, 1991.

Lydia Dotto
Ethical Choices and Global Greenhouse Warming. Waterloo, ON: Wilfrid Laurier University Press, 1993.

Gregg Easterbrook
A Moment on the Earth: The Coming Age of Environmental Optimism. New York: Viking, 1995.

Lynne T. Edgerton
The Rising Tide: Global Warming and World Sea Levels. Washington, DC: Island Press, 1991.

Friends of the Earth
The Rainforest Harvest: Sustainable Strategies for Saving the Tropical Forests? London: Friends of the Earth, 1992.

Al Gore	*Earth in the Balance: Ecology and the Human Spirit*. Boston: Houghton Mifflin, 1992.
John Gribbin	*The Hole in the Sky: Man's Threat to the Ozone Layer*. Rev. ed. New York: Bantam Books, 1993.
Christopher Joyce	*Earthly Goods: Medicine-Hunting in the Rainforest*. Boston: Little, Brown, 1994.
Gordon MacMillan	*At the End of the Rainbow? Gold, Land, and People in the Brazilian Amazon*. London: Earthscan, 1995.
Chico Mendes with Tony Gross	*Fight for the Forest: Chico Mendes in His Own Words*. Rev. ed. London: Latin America Bureau UK, 1992.
Patrick J. Michaels	*Sound and Fury: The Science and Politics of Global Warming*. Washington, DC: Cato Institute, 1992.
George J. Mitchell	*World on Fire: Saving an Endangered Earth*. New York: Scribner's, 1991.
David E. Newton	*Global Warming: A Reference Handbook*. Santa Barbara, CA: ABC-CLIO, 1993.
Annika Nilsson	*Greenhouse Earth*. New York: Wiley, 1992.
Michael Oppenheimer and Robert H. Boyle	*Dead Heat: The Race Against the Greenhouse Effect*. New York: BasicBooks, 1990.
Andrew Revkin	*Global Warming: Understanding the Forecast*. New York: Abbeville Press, 1992.
Nigel J.H. Smith et al.	*Tropical Forests and Their Crops*. Ithaca, NY: Cornell University Press, 1992.

Index

189